CREATION

THE PRINCIPLE OF NATURE IN ISLAMIC METAPHYSICS

CREATION

THE PRINCIPLE OF NATURE IN ISLAMIC METAPHYSICS

Erkan M. Kurt

15 14 13 12   1 2 3 4

Published by Blue Dome Press
244 Fifth Avenue #2HS
New York, NY 10001

www.bluedomepress.com

Library of Congress Cataloging-in-Publication Data Available

ISBN: 978-1-935295-18-1

Printed by
Imak Ofset Basim Yayin - Turkey

CONTENTS

PREFACE

Nature is the world we witness, the world we observe. But how does this world come to exist? From what ultimate cause does it spring into being? These are the fundamental questions that motivate metaphysical thinking, and they are answered here in the context of the Islamic metaphysical tradition. In this book, the Qur'anic discourse is employed as a frame of reference for the explanation of natural phenomena. This is not simply the speculative question of how the universe first emerged. The Islamic tradition seeks to illuminate the cause of the occurrence of natural events in every instance. What is sought is nothing less than the constant of existence, the principle that governs the perennial emergence of the world from the formation of stars to the movement of continents, from the wind as it blows to the rain as it falls, from the sprout of a seed to the ripening of fruit, from the birth of a person to the death of a culture. This principle is "creation," for every natural thing comes into existence through the creative command of God.

This understanding of "creation" in the fullest sense suggests that all nature, in all space, at all times is the effects of divine command. In Islam, this is also an expression of the principle of unity (*tawḥīd*) that acknowledges only one Creator and attributes all existence to His absolute wisdom. This Islamic notion of "creation" rejects the assumptions of naturalism, that nature is autonomous or contingent, and subordinates all of creation to the unity of the divine will. This anti-naturalistic worldview is embodied in the language of a Muslim's everyday life. The word "*bismillāh*" (in the name of God) begins every work; the word "*in shā' Allāh*" (if God wills) conditions the future. The prayers that are offered when departing on a trip, making a decision, yearning for rain; the thanks that is expressed in the face of an abundant crop, a significant coincidence, a pleasant success; these all express the Muslim's faith that God's creative command encompasses and determines the world at all levels of detail. Faith in creation's ultimate unity in the divine will informs the Muslim belief in "destiny" (*qadar*), perhaps best expressed by the words of a tablet that adorns traditional spaces: "What God says happens." Here we have a succinct formula of the principle of creation.

With this book, it is my hope that an examination of the Islamic principle of creation will offer a glimpse of the liberating potential of Islamic metaphysics against the groundless naturalism that has characterized the despair of modern times. For it is impossible to get rid of the hooks of nihilism without untying the knots of this naturalism. Here I argue that "creation" is the only humane principle of existence in that it answers the question, "Who am I, and what does this all mean?" uniquely in favor of the human individual. Teaching that existence in the world is by divine command, the principle of creation gives the corollary that existence will continue in a new nature after my death if I remain committed to the Creator in goodness. Providing a realistic vision of this good news comprises my primary hope as author. I would like to state my gratitude for all of those who contributed to the "coming into existence" of the book, especially my doctoral advisor Ilyas Celebi at Marmara University Divinity School in Istanbul, the dear friends from the "Hyde Park circle" of natural philosophy in Chicago, and my language and style editor Alex Dupree. I praise and thank God, who has bestowed upon me my humanity, for bringing this book into existence. I pray that it would be useful in our metaphysical quest.

INTRODUCTION

"Nature" is the observed world, also called the phenomenal world or the world of phenomena. In contemporary language, "nature" typically refers to the world that we see: the entire landscape of the existence from the earth to the heavens.[1] This is a revealing philosophical derivation from the original meaning of the word. Although "nature" originally denoted "essence" or "disposition," as is the case when we still speak of "the nature of something," the word came to refer in modern philosophical language to the external world as it appears.[2] This transition can be understood in three stages. First, "nature" was a name for the force intrinsic to material things. For Aristotle, the founder of natural science in the West, "nature" (*physis*) designated matter's innate potential for motion and change.[3] Aristotelian natural philosophers, many of them Muslim, elaborated on this basic definition.[4] Similarly, Muslim theologians defined nature as the specific created potential in things.[5] In the second phase of this etymology, the definition expanded to encompass not just force or potential in matter, but matter itself. Hence, all material things could be included in the category "nature." Ibn Sīnā, the prominent Peripatetic philosopher of the 11th century, stated that "nature" (*ṭabīʿa* in Arabic) includes all material and sensible things.[6] In a similar way, al-Ghazzālī, the great theologian of the 12th century, referred to the whole material world as the "world of nature" (*ʿālam al-ṭabīʿa*).[7] Finally, "world of nature" was simply shortened to "nature,"

---

1 Alfred North Whitehead, *The Concept of Nature*, 3.

2 See R. G. Collingwood, *The Idea of Nature*, 43.

3 Aristotle, *Physics* (ed. W. D. Ross), 348.

4 See Ibn Sīnā, *al-Samāʿ al-ṭabīʿī*, 99.

5 See Ibn Ḥazm, *al-Faṣl*, I, 15; Ibn Manẓūr, *Lisān al-ʿArab*, "ṭbʿa" entry.

6 Ibn Sīnā, *al-Ilāhiyyāt*, 21.

7 Al-Ghazzālī, *al-Munqidh min al-ḍalāl*, 86.

in the modern period. For instance, in the writings of Spinoza, the materialistic philosopher of the 17th century, "nature" is used to refer to the entire world of material things.[8]

When used to signify the whole of the observed world, the word "nature" fits comfortably into the language of every belief system. In Islamic terminology, "universe" (*al-'ālam*) denotes the entire world of creation and all its aspects, both observed and unobserved. This universe can be divided into two basic categories: the world seen (*'ālam al-shahāda*) and the world unseen (*'ālam al-ghayb*).[9] The former means "nature," and the latter "super-nature." The Qur'an distinguishes between what is in the scope of sight (*shahāda*) and what remains beyond (*ghayb*), making the latter subject to faith.[10]

Nonetheless, modern uses of the word "nature" are frequently intended to limit reality to the sensible world. In this view, the "universe" becomes synonymous with the traditional Islamic definition of "nature," and the possibility of existence's unobserved aspects is either denied or neglected. This kind of reduction is prevalent in contemporary scientific language, in which the word "universe" has become a strictly cosmological term.[11] Another naturalistic connotation portrays nature as an entity endowed with a fickle personality. This anthropomorphization of the external world is evident in phrases such as "gift of nature" and "nature's fault."[12]

The modern use of the word "nature" contains a revealing contradiction. Two very different meanings, the difference between "the nature of something" and "the realm of nature," compete directly in its adjective form: "natural."[13] "Natural" is primarily used in contemporary language to mean "pertaining to the observable world." But sec-

---

8 See James Collins, *God in Modern Philosophy*, 77.

9 See al-Baghdādī, *al-Farq bayn al-firaq*, 328; al-Āmidī, *al-Mubīn*, 99.

10 See Qur'an, 2:3, 33; 6:50, 73; 9:94, 105; 11:123; 13:9; 16:77; 23:92; 32:6; 39:46; 64:18.

11 As examples, consider the titles of these books from the literature of cosmology: Joseph Silk, *On the Shores of the Unknown: A Short History of the Universe*; Roger A. Freedman, William J. Kaufmann III, *Universe.*

12 Cf. John Habgood, *The Concept of Nature*, 3; Ivor Leclerc, *The Nature of Physical Existence*, 104.

13 See John Habgood, op. cit., 2.

ondary meanings suggest that the thing in question is "genuine," "inartificial," "unaffected," and "typical." These definitions all depend on the original, pre-modern meaning of the word. The contradiction here is that if everything that pertains to the world as it is observed is natural, then no observable thing can be unnatural. If this is the case, what is it that we attempt to designate with these secondary meanings? And why is it that we still call the artificial, humanly formed, and extraordinary things "unnatural?"[14] It is the contested position of the human being that the inconsistency reveals. Despite being a part of nature, none of the works of man, none of his exceptional experiences are designated as "natural." But if the human being is purely natural, why not his products as well? Which is more natural: a bird or its nest? A spider or its web?

It is clear that in modern usage, "nature" does not articulate a consistent notion. Today we say "the laws of nature" and "the beauty of nature" and refer to the modern understanding of nature as appearance, and then "the nature of humanity" or even "the nature of the world" utilizing the original definition of nature as essence. We speak of nature with a conceptual confusion peculiar to modern times.

To avoid unnecessary confusion in this book, I will adopt the following semantic restrictions. The word "nature" will refer, in its traditional Islamic usage, to the observable world that contains and surrounds the human being, the part of the universe that is "world seen." I will sometimes call it "the world" for short. I accept the older meaning of "nature" (i.e. essence, disposition) only in the grammar of "the nature of something." I mean "natural" only in its broader sense (i.e. pertaining to nature), and neglect "unnatural" thoroughly. As everything in the observable world is natural, the word "supernatural" becomes meaningless in reference to any phenomenon. When I write "natural event" or "natural process," I refer only to an event or a process in nature, such as the event of a sunrise or the process of a rain.

In the Qur'an, all natural events and processes are ultimately explained according to the principle of creation. As "the master of the worlds" (*rabb al-'ālamīn*) and "the creator of everything" (*khāliq kull shay'*), God realizes His will through His creative command, that is,

[14] See Herbert W. Schneider, "The Unnatural," 122.

through His imperative speech. This principle finds numerous references in the Qur'an:

> *To God belongs the sovereignty of the heavens and the earth and all that is between them. He creates whatever He will. God has power over everything.*[15]

To understand Islamic metaphysics, it is crucial to observe how the Qur'an explains God's sovereignty over the universe as His creative act of speech. A full elaboration of the principle of creation involves an understanding of the essence of God's creative command.

> *When He wills something to be, His way is to say, "Be," and it is.*[16]

This verse is repeated in various forms several times in the Qur'an, and I refer to all these instances together as the "verse of command." Here is an eloquent and figurative account of the ultimate origin of nature in the authority of God.[17] Islamic metaphysics uses this verse to affirm that every event in the universe occurs as a consequence of the divine command. In Islamic terminology, God's act of creation is *takwīn*, literally "bringing into being."[18] God's creative command (termed *al-amr al-takwīnī*) is distinguished from His religious and moral commands (termed *al-amr al-tashrī'ī*).[19] The result of the former is the material universe, whereas the result of the latter is the divine religion.

To explain the entirety of nature with the singularity of the divine command is to practice the principle of unity, *tawḥīd*, the most essential tenet of Islam. *Tawḥīd* means to acknowledge God as the only god, hence not to accept any creator other than Him.[20] In other words, the unity of divinity is expressed in the unity of His creative act. Thus, the will and power to create anything in the universe belongs to God

---

15 Qur'an, 5:17.
16 Qur'an, 36:82.
17 Cf. al-Rāzī, *Lawāmi' al-bayyināt*, 153.
18 See al-Nasafī, *al-Tamḥīd*, 28; 'Alī al-Qārī, *Sharḥ Kitāb al-Fiqh al-akbar*, I, 35.
19 See Bayāḍīzāda, *al-Uṣūl al-munīfa*, 48.
20 See al-Nasafī, *Baḥr al-kalām*, 21; al-Baghdādī, *al-Farq bayn al-firaq*, 338.

alone.[21] In the literature of classical theology, this creed is expressed by the famous sentence, "What God wills happens, and what He does not will does not happen."[22] The principle of creation thus addresses itself to the question of how any natural process comes into being at any time—not simply the question of how the universe emerged in the beginning. In this sense, "creation" explains the past, present, and future of nature with the same fundamental metaphysical tenet. It is this principle as a constant that gives form to all occurrences: the radiation of a star in the sky, the development of a baby in the womb, the establishment of peace in the society. In this sense, "creation" is not a term that relates to the history of nature or natural science. It means nothing to compare "creation" to any of the principles of these fields, nor is it possible to verify or falsify "creation" in the context of any historical or scientific theory.

In this sense, creation is principle common among the so-called Abrahamic faith traditions, namely Judaism, Christianity, and Islam. Each of these religions explains the existence of nature as the result of the creative command of God.[23] This mutual belief rejects the assumptions of modern naturalism. As a principle, naturalism considers the world to be autonomous, existing independently of a creator's will and power.[24] Interestingly, naturalism does not contradict the plain sense of the word "creation." Regarding its simple meaning "to create," the word can refer to the substantial coming into being of nature, and this substantial existence is undeniable. In naturalistic literature, nature's origins, from the formation of the universe to that of living species, are often referred to by the term "creation," and the consequent components of nature are referred to as "creatures."[25] Thus, neither a meta-

---

[21] Cf. al-Māturīdī, *al-Tawhid*, 21; Ibn Abū al-'Izz, *Sharḥ al-'Aqīda al-Ṭaḥawiyya*, 25.

[22] In Arabic: "*Mā shāa'llāhu kāna wa mā lam yasha' lam yakun.*" See al-Baghdādī, *Uṣūl al-dīn*, 102; Ibn Taymiyya, *al-Qaḍā wa al-qadar*, 87; Izmirli, *Muḥaṣṣal al-kalām wa al-ḥikma*, 45.

[23] Don Cupitt, *Creation out of Nothing*, 6.

[24] See Roy Wood Sellars, *Evolutionary Naturalism*, 2.

[25] See, as examples, Barry Parker, *Creation: The Story of the Origin and Evolution of the Universe*; Colin Tudge, *The Variety of Life: A Survey and A Celebration of All the Creatures that Have Ever Lived.*

physical nor a scientific understanding fully opposes "creation" in this plain sense. Moreover, as long as it is used in this plain sense, "creation" can by no means be verified or falsified. However, today we usually go further than such simple language and use "creation" to refer to the religious explanation of existence as the result of God's creative command. Therefore, one should distinguish in what sense the term "creation" is used in any discourse on nature.

This book is a treatise on the principle of creation that is taught in the Qur'an. It is an attempt to understand the creative command of God in terms of both essence and effect. The processes and dynamics of nature come into existence as the effect or result of God's creative command. This command is the absolutely powerful wisdom that encompasses and orders universal space, motivates and sustains physical processes, and thus brings nature into existence. This metaphysical principle applies at all times and to all levels of the natural world. Here, the doctrine of creation from classical Islamic theology is recast in contemporary language, definitively closing the gap between the essence and effect of the divine command. God's act of creation is fully equivalent to His command, and the divine command is a mode of the divine speech. These important notions seem to be neglected in the literature of classical theology, yet they illuminate the lively relation between God's nature and the natural processes of our world. Indeed the literature of classical theology includes no discourse on how divine wisdom and power are manifest in the world, or in what manner God brings various physical phenomena into existence. The answer to these theological questions also offers a solution to our most fundamental metaphysical curiosity: "How can we exist?"

Part One

THE FOUNDATIONS OF CREATION

1.

The Ultimate Explanation of Nature

As human beings, the reality of the world is one of our immediate assumptions. All of our statements ultimately assume that the world before us is tangible and true.[26] For this reason, classical Islamic theology begins its metaphysics with the affirmation of the truth of things.[27] This truth (*ḥaqīqa*) or essence (*māhiya*) is articulated in the basic definition of a given object. For example, when a human being is classically defined as the "thinking organism," this functions as a determination of the essential qualities that make a human being human. Similarly, the question, "What is the essential truth of the world?" is first of all an inquiry into the ultimate definition of "the world."

To understand what such a definition signifies, let us first consider the world as "appearance." If a film is projected into a two-dimensional screen, the world can be thought of as projected into the three-dimensional "universal space." Then the truth of the world corresponds not to something beyond it, but to the truth of its universal appearance. The world cannot be known apart from this appearance. But why this particular appearance? And how does it come to be before us? Here emerge the fundamental inquiries that challenge the apparent completeness of the world's existence. These questions move from consideration of the world's apparentness to contemplation of the reason for its appearance. "What ultimately ensures the

---

[26] See Jan Westerhoff, *Ontological Categories*, 1 et seq.

[27] See al-Nasafī, *al-Tamḥīd*, 2; al-Taftāzānī, *Sharḥ al-'Aqāid*, 56.

universal appearance?" In other words: "On what source does the existence of the world depend?" At the same time this question radically opens the concept of "physic" as nature to inquiry, it transcends the limits of "physics" as natural science. It is the very definition of the world as mere appearance that inspires metaphysical speculation.[28]

As a field of study, metaphysics aims for the ultimate explanation of nature. Although "metaphysics" literally means "after physics," the categories of explanation it employs logically precede the methodologies of physics. Ibn Sīnā comments on this odd reversal:

> The sense of subsequence in the name "meta-physics" (*mā ba'd al-ṭabī'a*) is in the language only, because it is this natural existence by which we witness existence at first and only then do we inquire after its conditions. This science deserves the name of "before-physics" (*mā qabl al-ṭabī'a*) since its subjects actually are prior to physics.[29]

In Aristotle's work, in which the term "metaphysics" originates, posthumous editors attached the prefix "*meta*" (after) to the chapters that followed the numerous chapters on "*physis*" (nature). Thus the elements of the "first philosophy" as elaborated by Aristotle came to be called "after nature." This attribution preserves in a particularly telling way the curious relationship between the ultimate cause and the appearance of the world. Unless we begin by taking nature at the level of appearance, we cannot discern the ultimate explanation of its origin. It is then meaningful that metaphysics comes after physics in terms of study; even though the former logically must precede the latter.

Metaphysics seeks to articulate the ultimate explanation of the world, and this effort is inseparable from humanity's basic desire to understand itself. There is no way to understand humanity apart from the nature that contains and surrounds us. This desire for self-knowledge is characteristic of humanity and provides a perpetual impetus for metaphysical thinking.[30] Moreover, this desire for an ultimate

---

[28] Cf. Bruce Aune, *Metaphysics*, 3 et seq.; W. T. Stace, *The Nature of the World*, 3.

[29] Ibn Sīnā, *al-Ilāhiyyāt*, 21.

[30] Cf. Peter Loptson, *Reality: Fundamental Topics in Metaphysics*, 10; Robert M. Torrance, *The Spiritual Quest*, 1; George P. Adams, *Man and Metaphysics*, 44.

explanation expresses our basic concern with the sacred: if the absolute origin on which nature's existence depends cannot be located within the natural world, if it transcends it, then this origin acquires sanctity.[31] In this regard, the history of metaphysics is also the history of the quest for the sacred truth on which nature ultimately depends.

In the literature of metaphysics, the ultimate explanation of nature arises as an answer to four perennial human questions. *Why is there something instead of nothing?* As the most fundamental curiosity about the truth of the world, this is the question of "existence" (*wujūd*, in Islamic terminology). *Why did nature come into being and why does it continue?* Inquiring as to the goal and meaning of the world, this is the question of "purpose" (*ghāya*). *How did nature come into being and how does it continue?* Seeking to understand the way of the existence of the world, this is the question of "principle" (*mabda'*). *Is nature finite, and is there anything beyond death?* This question, reflecting the ultimate concern of the human being in the world, is the question of the "end" (*ma'ād*).[32] To summarize, the fundamental desire for ultimate explanation can be expressed in a single question: "Who am I, and what is the meaning of all this?"[33] This touch point of metaphysical thinking is a basic expression of the human individual's desire to learn his or her ultimate identity. From another perspective, it is the appeal of the mortal to the surely immortal source of existence. In this way, the metaphysical quest constitutes the essence of religious orientation.[34]

An appeal to the ultimate reality that is the origin of nature is an appeal to infinity, for the ultimate reality must be the eternal reality. That is, the truth that ultimately sustains the existence of a finite world cannot itself be finite. Reality does not depend on nothingness; truth does not arise from naught. Thus the reality of nature as appear-

---

[31] Cf. Seyyed Hossein Nasr, *Knowledge and the Sacred*, 133.

[32] For essential metaphysical questions, see Arthur Witherall, *The Problem of Existence*, 2; Milton K. Munitz, *The Mystery of Existence*, 4; Karl Britton, *Philosophy and the Meaning of Life*, 3.

[33] Cf. Gabriel Marcel, *Problematic Man* (tr. Brian Thompson), 19.

[34] See Alfred Adler, *Understanding Human Nature* (tr. Walter Beran Wolfe), 263.

ance necessarily proves an eternal reality that could cause it.[35] In Islamic metaphysics, this eternal reality has received the title "*al-wājib al-wujūd*," or "the One whose existence is necessary."[36] This terminology suggests an inevitable equation: Whatever name may be given to the ultimate reality that lies beyond the appearance of nature, this ultimate ground logically corresponds to the sense of the eternal reality that Islam designates with the name "God."[37] In Arabic, "*Allāh*," the name that denotes the Creator of the heavens and the earth, is a derivation from the original "*al-ilāh*," which precisely refers not to a proper name, but to a concept: "the God"[38] The equivalence between the proper name "God" and the concept of an "eternal reality" can be observed in translation. Translation is only possible between semantically equivalent words, and it is the more general concept of an "eternal reality" inherent in the proper name "God" that allows for the name's translation into many languages.[39]

The logical necessity of an eternal reality suggests two things: (1) Since the origin of nature is ultimately this eternal reality, "God" is a necessary concept and "divinity" is an essential category for metaphysics. In other words, it is impossible to do metaphysics without appealing to some form of the idea of "God." Metaphysics is thus necessarily founded on the basis of "theology," the study of divinity. This is why Aristotle, who cited metaphysics as the "first philosophy," also called it "theology."[40] Likewise, Ibn Sīnā entitled his metaphysical work as "Theology" (*al-Ilāhiyyāt*) and remarked that God is the necessary subject of metaphysics.[41] (2) Since the existence of nature necessarily implies an origin in an eternal reality, namely "God," then the existence of "God" in this sense cannot be a matter of controversy. To

---

[35] Cf. al-Juwaynī, *al-Irshād,* 21; al-Āmidī, *Abkār al-afkār*, I, 227; F. H. Bradley, *Appearance and Reality*, 236.

[36] See al-Fārābī, *Fuṣūṣ al-ḥikma*, 56; Ibn Sīnā, *al-Najāt*, II, 89; al-Rāzī, *al-Mabāhith al-mashriqiyya*, II, 542.

[37] See Paul Weiss, *Being and Other Realities*, 35.

[38] See Ibn Manẓūr, *Lisān al-'Arab*, "alh" entry.

[39] See Michael Durrant, *The Logical Status of God*, 3 et seq.

[40] Aristotle, *Metaphysics* (tr. Hippocrates G. Apostle), 186; cf. R. G. Collingwood, *An Essay on Metaphysics*, 5.

[41] Ibn Sīnā, *al-Ilāhiyyāt*, 6.

argue concerning the existence of God in absolute sense (namely, to ask, "Does God exist?") is as meaningless as arguing whether or not the world exists. The only meaningful question is: "Who is God?" Here the problem is not one of existence but of identification. All metaphysical systems employ an idea of "God" in the sense of an absolute, eternal reality, what varies from belief to belief is the divine identity.

On the other hand, "divinity" categorically makes two things definite. First, all disagreements about the ultimate explanation of nature essentially arise from differences in the identification of God. Metaphysical controversies are thus revealed to be essentially theological. Second, if the ultimate explanation of nature must invoke the identity of God, then the world in general and the human being in particular cannot be ultimately defined until God is known.[42] The question "Who am I, and what is the meaning of all this?" cannot be answered until the question "Who is God, and what does He want from me?" is answered. In this case, the most significant question for the human individual aspiring to understand his or her ultimate identity is the question of the identity of God.[43]

To know God, an individual must appeal to a source of knowledge that would reveal His eternal identity. Such a source can be called a "theological reference," and of course what is theological is also by definition metaphysical. These source references are known as sacred texts or holy books, and the different theologies they espouse have been the cause of many metaphysical disagreements. However, all of these source texts share an attempt to respond to the human need for ultimate explanation. From this aspect, consideration shown towards sacred texts is completely a "human" phenomenon.[44] Still, this consideration does not rest on the fact that the sacred texts speak of God. Any text can do this. Instead, it rests on the fact that they provide "news" of God's identity or essence. The defining characteristic of a holy book is that it is regarded as being somehow "received from God" and is therefore read carefully as the "divine word."

---

[42] Cf. Descartes, *Principles of Philosophy* (tr. Valentine Rodger Miller and Reese P. Miller), 7.

[43] Cf. Rāghib al-Isfahānī, *Tafṣīl al-nash'atayn*, 61.

[44] Cf. Wilfred Cantwell Smith, *What is Scripture*, 212, 217.

A metaphysical system that has a sacred text as its frame of reference can be called a "scriptural metaphysics" or "religious metaphysics." It also deserves to be referred to as a "positive metaphysics," in that it relies on a source of positive knowledge, or "divine word," to instill the certainty of faith in its believers. As metaphysics of faith, these scriptural systems of belief are to be understood in contrast with "philosophical metaphysics" that rest on speculation. That is to say, without a sacred text to orient belief, the desire for understanding gives way to divergent speculation.[45] In the absence of a foundational text, philosophical metaphysics can be based either on logical deduction (rational metaphysics) or a blend of speculation with spiritual intuition (mystical metaphysics).

In its attempt to describe the ultimate truth, philosophical metaphysics fills the gap between divine authority and human capacity with speculation. Nevertheless, speculation does not ensure knowledge, for it is always accompanied by the possibility of error. In this way, a speculative metaphysical system ends by subverting the human desire for certainty whenever it reaches the limits of its legitimacy. This is the problem faced by all non-scriptural and non-positive metaphysics.

Modern analytic philosophy rejects the approach of speculative metaphysics, claiming that this approach has nothing to do with knowledge.[46] Wittgenstein, a pivotal figure in this field, suggests that speculative metaphysics has destined itself to failure and should henceforth remain silent.[47] The philosopher seems to imply that without a regarded source of knowledge, a valuable metaphysical system is impossible. So a human individual who aspires to learn his or her ultimate identity should remain silent until the source for such ultimate truth is obtained.[48] Is this silence possible? For Kant, one of the earliest philosophers to reject the speculative metaphysics, silence is

---

[45] Cf. Andrew J. Reck, *Speculative Philosophy*, 12; Richard Taylor, *Metaphysics*, 2, 5.

[46] See Immanuel Kant, *Prolegomena*, 13 et seq.

[47] Ludwig Wittgenstein, *Tractatus*, 151 (6.53).

[48] Cf. S. N. Hampshire, "Metaphysical Systems," 25, 28.

impossible and speculation cannot be avoided, just as it is impossible to give up breathing together to avoid inhaling impure air.[49]

It is safe to say that the sacred texts have suffered a loss of credibility in the modern period. The naturalistic metaphysics, sailing on the winds of science, has gained influence. Additionally, the secular character of modern life has paralyzed metaphysical sensitivity in the human individual. The prevalent discourse of modern life is almost exclusively the language of "physic," which limits reality to what is measurable and sensible.[50] In this context, the questions of ultimate meaning wither away, and belief recedes to shallow shoals of life.[51] The question "What does this natural event ultimately *mean*?" is a concern that should either be forgotten or endlessly deferred. I prefer to denote such an attitude of forgetting and deferring as "appearantialism." It is an attempt to sever meaning from nature through a fixation on the appearance of the world.

The "appearantialist" greets the rainfall only with the topside of an umbrella, remaining indifferent to the religious or metaphysical meaning of the event. When going to sleep, the appearantialist does not meditate on the meaning of sleep, or about what the sunlit morning ultimately reveals. In this respect, "appearantialism" is a forgetful naivete, like the child who indulges in trifles to forget his or her duty. It is a fascination with appearance that resembles bewitchment, and it is in this forgetful state that Descartes, the founder of modern philosophy, finally restricted his search for truth to the realm of physics, stating, in the conclusion of his book, that he would dedicate the rest of his life to the obtainment of knowledge of nature.[52]

---

[49] Immanuel Kant, *Prolegomena*, 116.

[50] See Rene Guenon, *The Crisis of the Modern World* (tr. Marco Pallis et al), 81 et seq.

[51] Cf. Seyyed Hossein Nasr, *Man and Nature*, 17, 18.

[52] Descartes, *Discourse on the Method* (tr. George Heffernan), 105.

2.

Naturalism against Creation

As a metaphysical position, naturalism typically assumes nature to be independent of supernatural influence. This view can be traced back to the attitude of the appearantialist. Dedicating his gaze to the appearance of the world, the appearantialist can conceive of nothing beyond it. When appearance veils the ultimate reality and absorbs the whole meaning of the world, nature looks as if it were free and independent. A fisherman caught in a storm, for instance, forgets in his terror the ultimate meaning of the storm, and the existence of the waves and the gales, in their appearance, confront him as independent forces. The naturalistic principle is this very supposition of independence that originates in the appearantialistic bewitchment. Al-Ghazzālī warns against the charm of appearance in philosophy:

> It is essential to know that nature is subservient to God. It does not function according to its own merit, but is employed by its Creator. The sun, the moon, the stars, everything is subservient to His command. None of these things act unless He first acts.[53]

Al-Ghazzālī's warning is targeted especially against the Aristotelian naturalism manifest in the philosopher's argument that the world is eternal, ungenerated, and indestructible.[54] With this, Aristotle teaches that the world sustains its existence according to its own necessity,

---

[53] Al-Ghazzālī, *al-Munqidh*, 96.

[54] Aristotle, *On the Heavens* (tr. W. K. C. Guthrie), 83, 94.

independent of any divine source.[55] This is a critical point in his metaphysics, for an existence that is necessary, infinite, and independent is recognized by Islamic theology to belong uniquely to God.[56] In contrast, Aristotle attributes a divinity to nature in the same manner as his contemporary naturalists. He assumes nature to possess an independent authority distinct from God, as is apparent in his formulation, "God and nature create nothing that does not fulfill a purpose."[57] This sort of naturalism distributes divine qualities between God and the physical universe. In Islamic terms, this is equivalent to *shirk*: associating any partner with God.[58] The metaphysics of creation and of naturalism oppose each other on this principle of nature's independence. While the former considers nature to be absolutely dependent on God's will, the latter inevitably deifies nature by attempting to confer to it independent status.

Thus far, two predominant categories of naturalist metaphysics have emerged. "Practical" naturalism is unaware of the will of God and ignorant of the perennial creation of the world; and "theoretical" naturalism actively recognizes nature as independent of creation. The appearantialistic naivete mentioned above could be thought of as practical naturalism, whereas theoretical naturalism denotes an appearatialism reinforced by a certain conceptual framework. Practical naturalism neglects the principle of creation with neglect, theoretical naturalism negates it. As an everyday appearantialistic bewitchment, practical naturalism arises precisely from a lack of reflection and so does not need to be nurtured by philosophy. On the other hand, the theoretical naturalism engages in philosophical speculation beyond everyday behavior (though not beyond nature), and develops into a properly metaphysical worldview.

In practical naturalism, the everyday aspects of the world available for immediate use absorb attention, and inquiry into the meaning

---

55 See R. G. Collingwood, *The Idea of Nature*, 82.

56 See al-Rāzī, *Lawāmiʿ al-bayyināt*, 226; al-Bājūrī, *Tuḥfa al-murīd*, 50; al-Laqānī, *Itḥāf al-murīd*, 77, 80.

57 Aristotle, *On the Heavens*, 31.

58 Cf. ʿAbduh, *Risāla al-tawḥīd*, 62; Said Nursi, *al-Mathnawī*, 39; Fazlur Rahman, *Major Themes of the Qur'an*, 67.

of nature disappears from view. For a practical naturalist, the relation of the world to the divine will has essentially been forgotten. In this preoccupation with immediacy, nature is estranged from the divine sovereignty that animates it, and the human individual becomes simply a subject among autonomous objects. Practical naturalism counsels the human individual to fend for itself in this "world of livelihood," where an unceasing struggle for life prevails.[59] Whether enjoying the pleasures of life or struggling with the worries of survival, the individual cannot afford to pause and contemplate his mortality. To speak of the ultimate meaning of life is as untimely and improper for practical naturalism as it would be to ask a soldier in mid-combat how gunpowder was invented. Thus the practical naturalist shoulders an absolute paradox: the sole purpose of life is to stay alive. In this paradox, the only advantage that the human individual has over the animal is the use of practical reason. But reason is now reduced to a tool for survival, and the destruction of death will ultimately reduce even this advantage to nothing.[60] In the final analysis then, practical naturalism is the story of how a human being is ultimately devalued by the bewitchment of appearance.

The story of theoretical naturalism is longer and more conceptually sophisticated. "Nature" is no longer understood as the immediate field of survival, but a theorized, independent object to be observed and apprehended. By positing nature as independent in this way, the naturalistic philosophy inevitably makes the human being external to nature, conceiving of it as akin to a mother's bosom rather than a divinely bestowed home. The attribution of "motherhood" to nature is common in the tradition of naturalistic philosophy. With this language, the natural world is compared to a woman giving birth to related yet distinct creatures. And as "children of nature," humans are meant to replace reverence for the divine with reverence for the nurturing physical world. This imagery can be witnessed in many naturalistic discourses. For instance, the ancient Roman poet and philosopher Lucretius describes nature as a creative goddess and a majestic moth-

[59] Cf. S. Morris Eames, *Pragmatic Naturalism*, 42.

[60] Cf. Ibid, 41.

er.[61] For Montaigne, the humanistic author of the Renaissance, nature is nothing less than a mother who behaves compassionately towards humanity.[62] For Goethe, an Enlightenment naturalist, nature is a glorious goddess-mother deserving of our reverence.[63] Similar depictions can be found in contemporary naturalistic literature: the world is a goddess and nature her body.[64] Some Christian naturalists even refer to the earth itself as a child of God's.[65]

The different modes of this theoretical or "philosophical" naturalism attribute to nature various degrees of independence. Absolute naturalism considers nature to be completely independent: its own infinite reality. Hence it relates to nature as to an absolute divinity. With nature as its only reality, absolute naturalism cannot avoid putting nature in the God's unique place. This is the most extreme speculative variant of naturalistic thought. This "atheistic naturalism" utterly opposes the idea of the sublime Creator. It is not a disbelief that refuses to recognize God, instead it is a belief that misrecognizes nature as God. In this belief, nature itself acquires many divine attributes. "Nature" becomes a proper name, and the idea of an exalted God beyond this all-encompassing "nature" is condemned by such as Nietzsche as slander. For the German philosopher, what belongs rightfully to nature has been usurped by the idea of a Creator.[66] His argument can be summarized as: "I believe that there can be no god but Nature." Spinoza, in his metaphysics, also deifies nature, using "God or Nature" (*Deus sive Natura*) interchangeably in order to eliminate any misunderstanding.[67] It is strange that Einstein, Spinoza's philosophical successor, has been misunderstood due to his omission of the second part of this phrase. When Einstein speaks of "God" in his religious discourse, it is sometimes assumed that he is making reference to a sub-

---

[61] Lucretius, *On the Nature of the Universe* (tr. Sir Ronald Melville), 21, 67.

[62] See Montaigne, *The Essays of Montaigne* (tr. E.J. Trechmann), 1946.

[63] Rudolf Otto, *Naturalism and Religion* (tr. J. Arthur Thomson, Margaret R. Thomson), 25.

[64] See Mary Grey, *Introducing Feminist Images of God*, 76.

[65] See Karl E. Peters, *Dancing with the Sacred*, 144.

[66] James Collins, *God in Modern Philosophy*, 265.

[67] Ibid, 70.

lime Creator. But his "God" is not a transcendent being but rather a deification of natural processes.[68] The absolute naturalism opposes only the idea of a sublime God, not the idea that God is simply a name for the totality of the natural world. The popular atheistic naturalist Richard Dawkins states, in a book attacking belief in the Creator, that he has no problem with any belief that deifies nature in the way that Einstein does.[69]

Absolute naturalism regards the components of nature as parts of a divine whole, and so it contains a distinctly pantheistic element.[70] In regard to the supposedly "infinite" essence of nature, two different pantheistic metaphysics emerge: materialistic pantheism and spiritualistic pantheism. The former asserts that the essence of nature is its materiality, and that the world as we know it is but the structured and intricate manifestation of inanimate material obeying unconscious laws. This pantheistic thought is also called "materialistic naturalism" or simply "materialism." The ancient atomistic philosophers were the earliest representatives of this metaphysical system. Among them, Democritus and Epicurus assumed that indivisibly small material particles formed the ultimate reality of the world.[71] This assumption has clearly had its representatives in modern times. However, more recent developments in physics have led to adjustments in the conceptual base of materialistic naturalism.[72] Today's materialism, often called physicalism, considers the fundamental functions described by particle physics to be the ultimate reality of nature. For example, Gerard 't Hooft, the Nobel laureate theoretical physicist assumes, as do many of his colleagues, quantum entities to be nature's essential, reductive truth.[73] On the other hand, another variant of modern materialism is the idea of the infinite change and material development that is expressed by the philosophical use of the term "evolution." Evolution-

---

[68] See Albert Einstein, *Ideas and Opinions* (tr. Sonja Bargmann), 41.

[69] Richard Dawkins, *The God Delusion*, 20.

[70] See Paul Harrison, *The Elements of Pantheism*, 7.

[71] M. N. Roy, *Materialism*, 58.

[72] William R. Dennes, "The Categories of Naturalism," 270.

[73] See Gerard 't Hooft, *In Search of the Ultimate Building Blocks*, 178.

ary naturalism relates the formation of the world to the development of its physical essence according to a deified set of natural laws.

As for spiritualistic pantheism, it replaces matter with spirit and assumes the ultimate reality of nature to be a mysteriously conscious substance. The spiritualistic-pantheistic branch of Hindu philosophy is an example of this kind of naturalism. Here, everything is the divine manifestation of the spiritual and infinite substance called Brahman.[74] The concept of Logos in Western philosophy can be interpreted in a similar way. According to the philosophy of flux formulated by Heraclitus of Ephesus, the principle of the intellect, or "Logos," is the ultimate reality of the universe.[75] These spiritualistic pantheisms do not attempt to reduce the phenomena of consciousness, including the human soul, to matter in the way that materialism does. On the contrary, it relates matter to this spiritual substance and discards the dilemmas of materialism. Today some natural scientists favor Eastern spiritualism in a trend that can be thought of as a mystical variant of physicalism. While these scientists do not believe that a divine Creator determines the physical world, neither do they believe that matter is the ultimate ground of existence. These seemingly contradictory beliefs are an effort to combine the materialistic and spiritualistic approaches of absolute naturalism. Inspired by speculative aspects of quantum physics, the mystical physicalism asserts that the ultimate reality generating nature at the subatomic level will prove to be the absolute essence familiar from more ancient spiritualism.[76]

Now we come to the varieties of relative naturalism. These rest on the premise that nature is not absolutely independent; it is to a certain extent subject to the will of a sublime God. Deism is a famous example of relative naturalism. The Deistic philosophy regards God as the initial creator of the universe, but does not relate the ongoing existence of nature to God's sustaining will. Instead, God is assumed to have set up nature to function independent of His existence. Deism thus limits God's creative authority to the initial establishment of the universal order. An interesting example of this metaphysics is Plato's

---

[74] See Cybelle Shattuck, *Hinduism*, 27.

[75] Andrew J. Reck, *Speculative Philosophy*, 188.

[76] See Fritjof Capra, *The Tao of Physics*, 131.

narrative of cosmogony. In his imagining, a creator named Craftsman (Demiurge) builds the world in an artistic way and then ceases to disturb it, leaving it as the independent work of his hands.[77] In fact, most creation myths pattern such Deistic motifs.[78] Creation myths, comprising a significant part of the literature of mythology, describe the origin of nature in fantastic images and generally in a Deistic way that assumes the removal of the deity after the completion of creation.[79]

Since the 17th century, when science began to formulate explanations for the forces of nature, many natural philosophers in the West have adopted a Deistic attitude. The supposedly "mechanical order of nature," theorized by scientists such as Galileo, Boyle, and Newton, suggested a law-like world independent of supernatural influence. Nature was thought of as a closed system whose foundation had already been completed—an internally cohesive system not open to any external influence. The classical formulation compared the system of nature to a watch skillfully made: events took place according to predictable forces and determinate laws.[80] The Deists of the age of Enlightenment, philosophers such as Voltaire and Rousseau, denied God's creative authority in nature and paved the passage to the later atheistic philosophies of the modern world. For example, when Napoleon asked the French mathematician and astronomer Laplace why his book on the formation of the solar system made no mention of the Creator, he responded, "Sir, I had no need for such a hypothesis."[81]

Some contemporary religious movements have adopted "moderate" forms of Deism instead of embracing the full principle of creation. In these interpretations, God's absolute rule over nature is relativized until He becomes just a distant creator. This interpretation of Deism affirms the foundation of religious faith, yet asserts that the divine

---

[77] Plato, *Timaeus* (tr. Benjamin Jowett), 17 et seq.

[78] See Virginia Hamilton, *In the Beginning: Creation Stories from Around the World*.

[79] Cf. Charles H. Long, *Alpha: The Myths of Creation*, 18; Philip Freund, *Myths of Creation*, 16.

[80] See Richard S. Westfall, *The Construction of Modern Science: Mechanism and Mechanics*, 25 et seq.; Stephen Toulmin, *Cosmopolis: The Hidden Agenda of Modernity*, 110-113.

[81] Stanley L. Jaki, *God and the Cosmologists*, 32.

authority does not absolutely govern nature. In the course of its unfolding, nature is independent of God's command.[82] What naturalistic theologians offer here is more of a speculative confession than a scriptural one, limited by two apparent obstacles to the profession of God's absolute authority. First, physical laws offer an attractive portrait of nature as independently operative that leaves no room for the intervention of divine authority. Also, if nature were absolutely subject to divine authority, God must then be responsible for natural catastrophes and disasters. Deistic theologians worry that such responsibility would contradict God's absolute goodness. These are complicated problems for modern theology, and so some theologians tend towards a naturalistic metaphysics in an attempt to synthesize their theology with popular science.[83]

Another variant of relative naturalism is panentheism, which takes all of nature to be internal to the being of God. Originating in process philosophy, this idea does not consider God to be absolutely sublime. Instead, it suggests that God experiences a "becoming" in the world and is thus both super-natural and natural ("di-polar"). God is then not an absolutely perfect creator, but a creator who seeks perfection through manifestation.[84] The difference between panentheism and pantheism is that panentheism assumes only a partial, unfulfilled identity between nature and God. The panentheistic naturalism does not recognize nature to be a reality absolutely independent from God, but nor is God a reality absolutely independent from nature. According to Whitehead, a famous representative of this metaphysical belief, God and the world both transcend and participate in each other. God creates the world as the world creates God.[85] This belief thus excludes any conception of the absolute will and power of God as a sublime ruler. The creed of absolute divine creativity, "What God wills happens," is considered to be one of the typical misconceptions of traditional religion.[86] In certain Christian

---

[82] See David Ray Griffin, *Religion and Scientific Naturalism*, 15, 17.

[83] See Ian G. Barbour, *Religion and Science*, 102; Peter Forrest, *God without the Supernatural*, 85.

[84] See John W. Cooper, *Panentheism: The Other God of the Philosophers*, 165 et seq.

[85] Alfred North Whitehead, *Process and Reality*, 348.

[86] See Charles Hartshorne, *Omnipotence and Other Theological Mistakes*, 6, 17.

theologies, this metaphysical position is expressed as "Process Theism": the speculation that nature is the image of God appearing to humanity.[87] Another view imagines God to be the ground of the natural order and its integrity.[88] More fantastic speculations suggest that nature exists within God's particular space-time.[89]

The last example of relative naturalism is the philosophy of agnosticism. Keeping its distance from speculative metaphysics, agnosticism chooses not to imagine any ultimate explanation for nature without completely discarding it as a possibility. But even if divine creation were in fact the origin of the world, agnostics choose to restrict their attention to nature as the only reality that can be known. This position is not an outright denial of the sublime God, but a doubt that says, "Since I do not have any direct knowledge of this phenomenon, I can make no judgment about it." An agnostic suspends metaphysical speculation, assuming that nature as it appears is the only knowable reality. Agnosticism prefers an essentially naturalistic attitude, at least until another position is adequately proven.[90] David Hume, for example, objects to belief in the divine creation, asking, "Why can the material universe not be the necessarily existent Being?"[91] This question resonates with the objections of absolute naturalism: "Why must we think there is a god other than nature?" It is an indecisive form of atheism. Bertrand Russell, a hazy atheist in this way, was once asked why he rejected belief in God. His answer was very simple: "I should say that the universe is just there, and that is all."[92] This form of agnosticism sounds like a modernized version of an ancient naturalism. Throughout the ages, naturalism has not moved any further than this supposition. Rather than relinquishing a childish fixation on appearance, generations of naturalists have chosen instead to content themselves with it.

---

[87] Langdon Gilkey, *Nature, Reality, and the Sacred*, 175.

[88] Willem B. Drees, *Creation: From Nothing until Now*, 25.

[89] Arthur Gibson, *God and the Universe*, 95.

[90] See Milton K. Munitz, *The Mystery of Existence*, 175; Sterling P. Lamprecht, *The Metaphysics of Naturalism*, 180.

[91] David Hume, *Dialogues Concerning Natural Religion*, 100.

[92] See John Hick, *The Existence of God*, 175.

3.

The Critique of Naturalism

Such divergent metaphysical speculations seem unlikely to ever reach a consensus, for human beings are speculative and curious by their very nature. It is not likely that this proliferation of theoretical naturalisms will ever resolve itself. On the contrary, naturalism's long history suggests that such beliefs will exist as long as the appearantialistic bewitchment persists. In this case, the metaphysics of creation faces the perennial task of analyzing the different logics of naturalistic speculations in order to reveal their inherent impossibilities. This task occupied al-Ghazzālī, the champion of the metaphysics of creation, for a considerable part of his life. Here I will simply begin to draw the outlines of the critique of theoretical naturalism.

We can start by applying to naturalism the essential critique that analytic philosophy makes of speculative metaphysics: namely, the inquiry of legitimacy. Is there any way to verify the assumption that nature was and is independent of a supernatural creativity? That it is not created? On account of its alleged independence, nature is postulated to be infinite, but on what basis and with what right? Al-Māturīdī, one of the founders of Sunnī theology, writes that those who claim the infinitude of the universe compare unduly the unobservable to the observable. It is merely assumed that the present existence of the cosmos stretches infinitely into the past.[93] Ibn Ḥazm, the great Andalusian theologian of the 11th century, argues that naturalists conclude the infinity of the cosmos on the basis that we cannot observe its first cre-

[93] Al-Māturīdī, *al-Tawḥīd*, 30.

ation. But if observation is the only source of knowledge for naturalists, how can they know that the cosmos is infinite? Can this infinity be witnessed?[94] In this way, Islamic theologians have asked naturalism to give a justification for its assumptions, reminding it that the burden of proof rests on the claimant.[95] The critique that analytic philosophy makes against speculative metaphysics is no different.

But defenses of legitimacy are unusual in the literature of naturalistic philosophy. In fact, naturalists often do not recognize that their assumption of an independent world is an assumption, and therefore they have no idea how to verify it as such.[96] The reason is obvious: if observation is the sole criteria for knowledge, it is impossible to conclude simply from observation that nature is not created. Although appearance is immediate, appearance itself does not prove that what appears is ultimate. Kai Nielsen, a contemporary naturalist, admits in his book that the suppositions of naturalism are ultimately groundless; it is a game that he calls "fallibilism."[97] That is to say, if asked, "Why should you deny that nature is subject to creation?" a naturalist cannot help but reply, "Because I cannot play this game otherwise." The admitted arbitrariness of this assumption subverts the rigor that we demand from metaphysics and brings naturalism back to the level of assumption. A naturalist can never be sure that this preoccupation with appearance does not come at the expense of something that lies beyond it. And precisely because the arbitrariness of this assumption can lead to frivolous conclusions, naturalism is not a compelling position for those who take existential study seriously.[98]

Rather than addressing this question of legitimacy, the literature of naturalistic philosophy complicates the problem by introducing additional illegitimate speculations and pseudo-theories. These pseudo-scientific explanations cannot withstand an immanent critique of naturalism according to its own scientific methodologies. For example,

---

[94] Ibn Ḥazm, *al-Faṣl*, I, 10, 11.

[95] See Juwaynī, *al-Shāmil*, 238.

[96] See William Ray Dennes, *Some Dilemmas of Naturalism*, 21, 22; Michael Ruse, *Evolutionary Naturalism*, 3; Kai Nielsen, *Naturalism without Foundations*, 35-37.

[97] Kai Nielsen, *Naturalism without Foundations*, 25-26.

[98] Cf. Michael C. Rea, *World without Design*, 59.

the set of the evolutionary-naturalistic speculations about the emergence of the organic life on earth cannot be supported by the criteria established by the naturalistic approach.[99] The cosmological "prophecies" put forth about the future of nature suffer from a similar limitation. Such naturalistic projections, based on the assumption that nature operates in totally consistent independence, are fanciful attempts to "shed light" billions of years into the future or to "illuminate" the end of the world.[100] Another example of such pseudo-scientific speculation is the concept of "synchronicity" set forth by naturalistic psychologists to explain the phenomena of extremely meaningful coincidences or dreams that seem to reflect the course of life in advance.[101]

Underlying these fantastic pseudo-theories is the apparent desire to fill the speculative spaces typically reserved for the concept of divine authority. It is not unusual that common people take seriously these pseudo-theories as science, even though they function more accurately as a part of the "naturalistic mythology." Stephen Toulmin remarks that these pseudo-scientific narratives are simply new myths for modern times that fill the void left in the absence of popular metaphysical belief.[102] The most famous of these pseudo-scientific myths is the "Story of Evolution" that recounts the establishment of nature as the story of a deified materialistic naturalism. In this story, the Big Bang marks the beginning of a completely naturalistic adventure, which proceeded until the "lucky" emergence of human beings and their culture, and will continue until the "unlucky" termination of the universal order.[103] In this way, the story of an independent nature becomes another instantiation of the mythic genre of creation narratives.

---

[99] For those speculations, see A. I. Oparin, *The Origin of Life on the Earth* (tr. Ann Synge), 73 et seq.; Paul Davies, *The Fifth Miracle: The Search for the Origin of Life*, 52 et seq.

[100] For examples, see Richard Morris, *The Fate of the Universe*, 128 et seq.; Arnold Benz, *The Future of the Universe*, 140 et seq.

[101] For the theory of synchronicity, see C. G. Jung, *Memories, Dreams, Reflections* (tr. Richard and Clara Winston), 304 et seq.; F. David Peat, *Synchronicity: The Bridge Between Matter and Mind*, 5 et seq.

[102] Stephen Toulmin, "Contemporary Scientific Mythology," 71.

[103] See Eric Chaisson, *Epic of Evolution*, 47 et seq.; T. R. E. Southwood, *The Story of Life*, 7 et seq.

Another mode of argumentation prevalent in the naturalistic literature, which is illegitimate by its own standards, is the attempt to smuggle metaphysical persuasion into physics, disguising a personal conviction with a barrage of "facts." Such abuse of the scientific language manufactures a kind of illusion. For example: (1) "Some eminent scientists have no recourse to any deity in constructing a suitable cosmology."[104] This simple illusion slyly reduces the concept of God into the cosmological category. (2) "Nature's love of stripes and spots extends into the animal kingdom, with tigers and leopards, zebras and giraffes."[105] This sentence attributes willpower to nature, or at least independence, but it does not express the metaphysical assumptions that support such an attribution. (3) "Earth will not become unbearably hot for another billion years and the Sun itself not perish for at least another five billion years."[106] Here, the conviction that there is no creative authority over nature is presented as if it were scientifically provable.

Scientific discourse is clearly being misused when its methodology becomes a mask for naturalism's metaphysical assumptions. If nature is assumed to be the ultimate reality, then natural science cannot help but become a metaphysical endeavor. If science presents itself as the unique study of the knowable, then knowledge is confined to scientifically provable statements. The "scientism" that inevitably results from such naturalistic assumptions postulates an absolute incompatibility between knowledge and faith. According to this worldview, science and religion are destined to confrontation because of their divergent understandings of nature. As knowledge increases, faith is supposed to decrease, and as religion is strengthened, science is supposed to be threatened.[107] This oppositional paradigm has dominated the modern period to such a degree that physics has replaced theology as "the queen of the sciences."[108] Positive knowledge of nature is considered by scientism to be the most valuable acquisition, worthy of life's devotion.[109] According to Albert Einstein, positive knowledge is the extreme

[104] Joseph Silk, *On the Shores of the Unknown: A Short History of the Universe*, 3.

[105] Ian Stewart, *Nature's Numbers: The Unreal Reality of Mathematics*, 8.

[106] Eric Chaisson, *Epic of Evolution*, 437.

[107] See Ian G. Barbour, *When Science Meets Religion*, 11.

[108] Cf. Richard J. Coleman, *Competing Truths*, 14.

[109] See Carl Sagan, *The Demon-Haunted World*, 1 et seq.

limit of knowledge that human being can attain. As such, he was proud to dedicate his life and skills exclusively to physics.[110] Similarly, scientists today seek, as the most noble project of humanity, the description of nature's fundamental forces in a unified equation: "the theory of everything."[111] But if science considers itself to be the study of positive knowledge, it would be difficult to argue that modern science fits such a definition, given the speculative nature of modern scientific discourse. Today, to claim legitimacy with reference to science, it is necessary to qualify to "which science" you refer.[112]

Of course, there is a strong philosophy of science that opposes the presentation of personal worldviews as the study of positive knowledge. This philosophy considers science to be an instrument for obtaining objective knowledge of the world and for making life more convenient.[113] But science is not able to determine the ultimate meaning of the world, and thus it cannot operate as a guide to life.[114] In Wittgenstein's words, "even when all possible scientific questions have been answered, the problems of life remain completely untouched."[115] In describing facts, science simply makes a record of appearances and ceases to be science otherwise.[116] The ultimate meaning of the world always lies beyond science, precisely because science can concern itself only with observation. A science that recognizes this limitation does not pursue such a meaningless utopia as "the theory of everything." Such an equation, even if it were found, could not say anything about the ultimate meaning of nature, that is, "everything."[117] As Wittgenstein writes, it is a naive illusion peculiar to modernity to think that scientific descriptions are "explanations" of natural phenomena.[118] The ultimate explanations belong to a more fundamental field of

---

[110] Albert Einstein, *Ideas and Opinions* (tr. Sonja Bargmann), 37, 45.

[111] See Stephen W. Hawking, *A Brief History of Time: From the Big Bang to Black Holes*, 155, 175.

[112] Cf. Alex Rosenberg, *Philosophy of Science*, 8 et seq.

[113] See Peter Godfrey-Smith, *Theory and Reality*, 183.

[114] Cf. Karl Jaspers, *Philosophy of Existence* (tr. Richard F. Grabau), 10.

[115] Ludwig Wittgenstein, *Tractatus*, 149 (6.52).

[116] Cf. J. R. Lucas, *Space, Time and Causality*, 2.

[117] Cf. John Polkinghorne, *Beyond Science: The Wider Human Context*, 47 et seq.

[118] Ludwig Wittgenstein, *Tractatus*, 143 (6.371).

knowledge that is both beyond and before physics. This is the place for metaphysical thinking. And only here can a proper relationship between religion and science begin. Only when the physical and the metaphysical worldviews are held together in this way is the complementary fullness of "human life" possible.[119]

Naturalism has also abused the language of logic in the modern period. The so-called logical positivism or logical empiricism, which prevailed in early 20th century scientific discourse, attacked the logic of metaphysics on account of scientism. These neo-positivists made "verifiability" the new criterion of their logic. "Verifiability" assumes that a concept is genuine and a sentence is meaningful only if they refer to the observed world, since only what is observed is real. All concepts and statements failing this criterion are pseudo-concepts and pseudo-statements.[120] The neo-positivists claim that the observed world provides not only the content for observation, but the content for meaning as well, inferring that no meaning or truth can be found outside of "science." This path of inquiry concludes that metaphysics is meaningless and should be discarded from life.[121]

The neo-positivist attempt to disprove religious beliefs and metaphysical systems contains three major flaws. First of all, the positivist assumption unrightfully and senselessly reduces the world of phenomena to the world of physics, ignoring myriad human experiences that have no place in the framework of the positive sciences. Second, they do not see that metaphysics explicitly deals with a reality that contrasts the domain of appearance, synthesizing its concepts from fundamental and necessary *a priori* notions. They do not discern, for instance, that the concept of "God" signifies the "eternal reality" in logical analysis, and that the concept of "creation" essentially means "to bring into existence." Third, logical positivism denies the possibility of a metaphysics that is justified by references to the world of phenomena in the same way that scientism is. When the prophet's experience is regarded

---

[119] See Stephen Jay Gould, *Rocks of Ages*, 4.

[120] See Alfred Jules Ayer, *Language, Truth and Logic*, 35; Carl G. Hempel, "The Empiricist Criterion of Meaning," 108.

[121] See Rudolf Carnap, "The Elimination of Metaphysics through Logical Analysis of Language" (tr. Arthur Pap), 60 et seq.

as real, that is, in case of faith, religious expression is verified by reference to the same sphere of reality as science. Just as the legitimacy of the positive sciences rests upon the trust in the senses, the legitimacy of the heavenly religions rests upon the trust in the revelation.[122] Is there a principle more ultimate than "trust" in epistemology?

It is not surprising that naturalism, which has no category for human experience, ends up attacking the human spirit. This opposition to spirit is a common feature of modern discourse, but its history extends to the ancient philosophies. In *Machine Man*, the 18th century French physician and philosopher La Mettrie describes the human being as a very complex machine, reducing consciousness to a physiological function.[123] This description is characteristic of modern materialism, in which the human being consists of nothing immaterial and personality can be reduced to a neurological category.[124] The human being is thus reduced to an animal species and human identity to a biological acquisition.[125] Materialistic psychology, in its aspiration to make brain chemistry responsible for the human self, turns consciousness into a "fake shadow" ultimately grounded in a contingent series of chemical reactions. Unconscious and involuntary matter simply deceives itself through a false perception of consciousness and will. Here the materialistic naturalism collapses into absolute nonsense, stating consciously and willingly that there is no consciousness and will. Logically, such a predicate articulates nothing. A materialist ineptly ignores the "subject" that thinks and speaks about objects. Searching for the self in chemistry is as vain as looking for the camera in the picture—an impossible reduction.[126] This opposition erected between nature and the human spirit cannot go beyond this unsuccessful attempt to eradicate the self. The biggest obstacle faced by naturalism is in fact the human being, and this reveals its absurdity.[127]

---

[122] Cf. Basil Mitchell, *The Justification of Religious Belief*, 99, 104; John Hick, *Faith and Knowledge*, 170; William A. Cristian, *Meaning and Truth in Religion*, 5.

[123] Andrew J. Reck, *Speculative Philosophy*, 112.

[124] See Francis Crick, *The Astonishing Hypothesis*, 3.

[125] See Eric T. Olson, *The Human Animal*, 17, 27.

[126] Cf. Ralph Walker, "Transcendental Arguments against Physicalism," 78; Mario Bunge, *The Mind-Body Problem*, 13; A. D. Smith, "Non-Reductive Physicalism?" 225.

[127] See Roy Wood Sellars, *Evolutionary Naturalism*, 3.

Materialistic naturalism therefore devolves into a philosophy that is blind to human existence, even anti-human. It is, in Schopenhauer's words, the philosophy of the subject that forgets to speak of himself.[128]

It is strange that naturalism, tending as it does towards this opposition between nature and humanity (and siding ultimately with nature), has brought about a philosophy of life called "humanism." Naturalistic humanism proclaims "everything for the human being" but for all that does not care about the human individual. It mercilessly counsels man to be satisfied with a slight felicity that will fade away in death, offering nihilism to the man who desires eternity. The best answer it can muster to the cry "Why should I live?" is a desperate cliché: "For the society!"[129] But this response ridicules the individual. To devote a mortal life to a mortal society is to ask a candidate of nothing to sacrifice himself for another candidate of nothing. Many thinkers, including Tolstoy, are convinced that the humanistic philosophy amounts to little more than a foolish distraction from its own inevitable hopelessness.[130] As amusement proceeds, only boredom arises. "Existential depression" is modern psychology's name for this gloom that emerges when life is affirmed to be nothing but vanity. This depression, often masked by everyday occupations, is manifest in crises at the boundary of life.[131] Through such crises, the absolute paradox of "humanism" is clearly discernible. This awareness may instigate a revolt against naturalism in the individual called an "existential experience," often leading to religious orientation and involvement. At the boundary of nature, the human individual turns toward the only reality that can preserve life beyond its natural limits, namely, toward God.[132] The individual returns to his desire for meaning, aspiring to save his life by learning his ultimate identity. At this extreme, the bewitchment of appearance breaks down.

---

[128] Arthur Schopenhauer, *The World as Will and Representation* (tr. E. F. J. Payne), II, 313.

[129] See Alfred Adler, *What Life Could Mean To You: The Psychology of Personal Development* (ed. Colin Brett), 15 et seq.

[130] See Tolstoy, *Confession* (tr. David Patterson), 17 et seq.

[131] See Viktor E. Frankl, *Man's Search for Meaning* (tr. Ilse Lasch), 106 et seq.

[132] Cf. Patrick L. Bourgeois, *The Religious within Experience and Existence*, 56.

4.

The Metaphysical Discourse of the Qur'an

Such existential experiences awaken a person's desire to know God. But to gain this knowledge a person must appeal to a dependable theological reference that will introduce Him. The word "dependable" here suggests that sources presenting speculation instead of knowledge are of no help to a person seeking sacred knowledge. The purpose is to know and take refuge in God, not to make assumptions of Him. Thus the speculative philosophy fails to satisfy. Karl Jaspers, the renowned philosopher of the 20th century, questions the value of theological speculation: "We do not want possibilities; we want reality."[133] The literature of mythology cannot provide a reliable reference either, for this literature consists only of indefinite narratives compiled by anonymous imaginations.[134] On the contrary, a sacred book is attributed to the prophet's experience of revelation, and its authority is derived from this attribution. Revelation is the experience of suddenly facing God after a desperate search for Him.[135] In our metaphysical quest, the thirst for the ultimate truth cannot be quenched until we hear God speak. But having heard, we are satisfied with the truth and thirst no more.[136] This thirst for truth is our innate

[133] Karl Jaspers, *Philosophy of Existence* (tr. Richard F. Grabau), 61.

[134] See Lewis Spence, *Introduction to Mythology*, 15; Marie-Louise von Franz, *Creation Myths*, 2.

[135] Cf. Howard Root, "Metaphysics and Religious Belief," 79.

[136] Cf. Jacques Maritain, *A Preface to Metaphysics*, 8.

prayer, and revelation is God's response to it.[137] As humans, we long for the voice of God to speak to us, and so we are ready to consider a prophet's experience of revelation.

In Islamic faith, the Qur'an provides an absolute reference for the ultimate meaning of the world. Revealed to the Prophet Muhammad (peace be upon him), this text is the Creator's speech to humanity. The Qur'an is considered by Muslims to be the word of God in the perfect sense, containing only divine speech. Faith that divine speech was indeed preserved in the Qur'an is bolstered by historical observations. First, the Qur'an's literary merit is unprecedented among contemporaneous Arabic traditions. Also, its religious teachings remarkably transcend its historical context. The proclaimer of the text, Muhammad of Mecca, was well known throughout his life to be a man of faith, truthfulness, integrity, honesty, sobriety, dignity, and modesty, and even displayed many miracles. Finally, this text has been duplicated diligently since its original revelation by means of professional scribing and memorization.[138]

One significant characteristic of the Qur'an is its mode of direct address. In the grammatical structure of the Qur'an, God presents Himself as "the Lord of the worlds" and "the Creator of the heavens and the earth" and addresses the Prophet as "the messenger," the society of the time, and all humankind. For a Muslim, reading or listening to the Qur'an is equivalent to hearing God's direct speech. Receiving God's words through the Qur'an is like receiving an imperial order from an envoy. In the following verses, for example, God addresses the listener:

> *We shall admit those who believe and do good deeds into Gardens beneath which rivers flow, there to remain for ever: a true promise from God. Who speaks more truly than God?*[139]

---

[137] Cf. Basil Mitchell, *The Justification of Religious Belief*, 42.

[138] For these foundations, see al-Bāqillānī, *I'jāz al-Qur'ān*, 33-80; al-Bayhaqī, *Dalāil al-nubuwwa*, I, 10-19; al-Ṣābūnī, *al-Bidāya*, 47-53; al-Rāzī, *al-Nubuwwāt*, 189-190.

[139] Qur'an, 4:122.

> *O mankind! The Messenger has come to you with the truth from your Lord, so believe, that is best for you. If you disbelieve, to God belongs all that is in the heavens and on earth. God is all knowing and all wise.*[140]

> *Behold this Book We have sent down to you so that you may bring people, by their Lord's permission, from the depths of darkness into light, to the path of the Almighty, the Praiseworthy One.*[141]

This language of direct address puts the reader of the Qur'an in the same position as the Prophet, and the text becomes the divine speech: an absolutely dependable source of knowledge. As Wilfred Cantwell Smith observes, believing in what the Qur'an says takes the form of witnessing to it.[142]

> The so-called "creed" of the Muslims is not a *creed* at all, if by creed one means an affirmation of belief. It is, rather, explicitly a "bearing witness" (*shahadah*). The Muslim does not say, I believe that there is no god but God, and I believe that Muhammad is the apostle of God. Rather, he asserts: "I bear witness to" these facts. His regarding them as facts, not theories, as realities in the universe not beliefs in his mind, is of quite basic significance.[143]

The Qur'an presents itself as a perfect and authoritative explanation of the world's ultimate meaning. It is offered as "guidance for people" and an "explanation for everything"; its text is "enlightening" and "perfectly explicit."[144] The Qur'an defines itself as a "light."[145] In commenting on this metaphor, al-Ghazzālī writes that the Qur'an is the light that makes unseen reality observable.[146] Besides, the Qur'an claims to be *al-ḥakīm,* or "the one that always judges wisely" and *al-furqān*, or "the one that perfectly differentiates between true and false."[147] In metaphysical terms, the Qur'an adopts the divine capacity

---

[140] Qur'an, 4:170.

[141] Qur'an, 14:1.

[142] Wilfred Cantwell Smith, *Faith and Belief*, 45.

[143] Ibid, 42.

[144] Qur'an, 2:185; 5:15; 12:1; 15:1; 16:89; 26:2; 27:1; 28:2.

[145] Qur'an, 42:52.

[146] Al-Ghazzālī, *Mishkāt al-anwār*, 12.

[147] Qur'an, 3:58; 5:48; 6:114; 10:1; 25:1; 31:2; 36:2.

for absolute wisdom and judgment which extinguishes ignorance regarding the ultimate meaning of the world. Through this word, God comes to the aid of the human mind caught up in appearance. Now there is no excuse for favoring the charm of appearance over the meaning of the world. Metaphysical controversies that stem from fantasy and speculation can now be judged against the divine explanation, and false conceptions can be definitively rejected.

The function of the Qur'an as a definitive reference forms the methodological basis for Islamic metaphysics. By appealing to the discourse of the Qur'an, the ultimate explanation of nature can be obtained positively and without speculation. This methodology has to assume that the Qur'an explains nature in an ultimate sense, revealing the meaning of natural events beyond what can be determined through observation. In other words, the Qur'an offers neither "natural history" nor "natural science." It is concerned solely with metaphysics, silently leaving physics to the human study of positive knowledge. For instance, the Qur'an describes the events of rainfall and of the revival of the earth in order to articulate the truth of the divine will and the final resurrection:

> *He is the One who sends the winds, bearing good news of His coming grace, and when they have gathered up the heavy clouds, We drive them to a dead land where We cause rain to fall, bringing out all kinds of crops. Thus shall We bring out the dead. Will you not reflect?*[148]

The essence of the Qur'an's metaphysical teaching is the principle of creation. The Qur'an answers the question, "Who am I, and what is the meaning of all this?" on the basis of this principle. This answer can be summarized according to the four essential questions of metaphysics mentioned above: First, it is the infinite reality of the Creator that explains why there is something rather than nothing: the existence of nature is the result of His will.[149] Second, nature was and is created so that the sublime values of the Creator could be known and acknowledged in worship and morality.[150] Third, nature was and is brought

[148] Qur'an, 7:57.
[149] See Qur'an, 2:255; 3:2.
[150] See Qur'an, 11:7; 51:56; 67:2.

into existence by the effect of the wise and powerful command of the Creator.[151] And fourth, nature will be brought to an end by the divine command, and a new and eternal nature will be established. Every individual will be recreated and revived again, to be judged and rewarded according to the divine mercy and justice and live immortally, either in the land of prosperity or in the realm of loss.[152]

The Qur'an expounds this metaphysical framework by extensively introducing the sublime Person of the Creator. Over the course of thousands of verses, the Qur'an presents the character of God in gorgeous rhetoric and gives clarification to various theological disagreements. The Qur'an speaks of a Creator who is one and unique, reminds us of the meaning and value apparent in creation, and specifies the divine will that realizes such creation. There is no intention "to prove the existence of God," that is, to verify the existence of the Creator through deductions from creation. In fact, the Qur'an does not practice this kind of "natural theology." From the standpoint of the Qur'an, this would be like trying to force an open door. Since "creation" is apparent, then the proper question is to ask of the identity or nature of the Creator, not whether the Creator exists. The proper question, according to the Qur'an, is: To whom does divinity belong?

> *Say: Praise be to God and peace on the servants He has chosen. Who is better: God or those they set up as partners with Him? God, who created the heavens and earth, and who sends down water from the sky for you, with which We cause gardens of delight to grow. You have no power to make the trees grow in them. Another god beside God? No! But they are a people who swerve from justice. God, who has made the earth a stable place to live, who made rivers flow through it, and who set immovable mountains on it and created a barrier between the fresh and salt water. Another god beside God? No! But most of them do not know. God, who answers the distressed when they call upon Him, who removes their suffering, and who makes you successors in the earth? Another god beside God? Little notice you take! God, who guides you through the darkness on land and sea and sends the winds as heralds of good news before His mercy. Another god beside God? God is far above the partners they put beside him! God,*

[151] See Qur'an, 2:117; 6:73; 16:40; 19:35; 36:82.

[152] See Qur'an, 81:1-14; 82:1-5; 84:1-15.

> *who originates creation and reproduces it, and who gives you provision from the heavens and earth. Another god beside God? Say: Show me your evidence then, if what you say is true.*[153]

The Qur'an begins its metaphysics with the statement: "There is no god but God." Faith in the unity of God, called *tawḥīd*, is the most essential aspect of Islam.[154] The Qur'an subsequently introduces the transcendent Personality of the Creator, identifying and praising His divine attributes—what are referred to as the "most beautiful names" (*al-asmā' al-ḥusnā*).[155] The Qur'an teaches that the obvious values of creation (such as orderliness, neatness, beauty, elegance, convenience, etc.) indicate the praiseworthy attributes of the Creator: His divine wisdom, power, beauty, mercy, compassion, grace, and generosity. Out of these attributes arise the divine "names": the Wise, the Powerful, the Beautiful, the Merciful, the Compassionate, the Graceful, the Generous, and so on. In the language of the Qur'an, qualities of creation are "signs" that point to the ultimate reality of the Creator.[156]

The meaningful creation of nature offers the potential for constant "remembrance" (*dhikr*), for creation will always bear the mark of its Creator's personal qualities.[157] The remembrance that nature facilitates in this way brings about a metaphysical sensitivity and awareness of the unseen and helps the individual to live in constant consciousness of God's unity. This consciousness is the foundation of Islamic morality. In the moral tradition, consistent with the Prophet's practice, there are numerous expressions for the remembrance of God in the course of everyday life. "*Bismillāh*" (In the name of God) is said at the beginning of any activity. "*Subḥānallāh*" (Glorious is God) marks any significant occurrence. "*Al-ḥamdu lillāh*" (Praise to God) expresses thankfulness for goodness and blessing. "*In shā' Allāh*" (If God wills) subordinates future events to the single will of God. "*Mā shā' Allāh*" (God has willed it) expresses in appreciation for any great happening. "*Ḥasbunallāh*" (God is sufficient for us) fortifies

[153] Qur'an, 27:59-64.
[154] See Ismail R. Faruqi, *al-Tawhid*, 18.
[155] See Qur'an, 7:180; 17:110; 20:8; 59:24.
[156] See Qur'an, 2:164; 3:190; 15:75; 45:5.
[157] Bk. Qur'an, 3:41; 16:13; 26:227; 40:13.

the speaker in difficult conditions. Such a pervasive remembrance of God connects the finite existence of the human individual to the infinite existence of the Creator. This speech disrupts the expectations of practical naturalism and protects against a theoretical naturalism that can drift into nihilism. The life of the Prophet (peace be upon him) was characterized by a perpetual attitude of remembrance to God, as the biographical literature on his life abundantly demonstrates.[158] Even at the hour of death, his preference for an exceptional expression of remembrance provided a splendid epilogue to his life of dedication. Having arrived at the boundary of nature, he turned toward the transcendent presence of God and with his last breath repeated: "O God, with the supreme communion."[159]

[158] For the examples of the Prophet's practices of remembering God, see al-Nawawī, *Ḥilya al-abrār*, 45 et seq.

[159] Ibn Hishām, *al-Sīra al-nabawiyya*, IV, 267; Ibn Ḥibbān, *al-Sīra al-nabawiyya*, 400.

Part Two

THE DIVINE COMMAND AS THE SOURCE OF NATURE

I.

God's Creative Will

1. The Determination of Nature by the Divine Will

God must will the existence of creation before He commands it. The divine command is therefore a voluntary act dependent on the divine will. In the Qur'anic verse of command, the phrase "*When He wills something to be*" testifies to this fact. The ultimate cause of nature's existence is the will of the Creator. This principle of creation can be translated into an expression of divine unity: in as much as this will is unique to God, the existence of nature absolutely depends on the divine will as its unique, single origin.[160] If "creation" is understood in its everyday sense (that is, as "coming into existence in meaningful way"), then nature clearly exists according to a creative will. In other words, "to create" necessarily implies a prior action of the will. The phrase "involuntary creation" is as meaningless and impossible as the phrase "involuntary art." Therefore, the meaningful existence of nature must refer to an original creative will.

An action of will is necessary for the creation of nature. In this way, the classical theologians simply refer to the existence of nature as evidence for God's will, without need for any further argument.[161] From this perspective, materialistic naturalism is founded upon an irreconcilable logical gap: it is the attempt to explain the existence of nature without referring to any creative intentionality. Arguments for "creative chance" in the discourse of evolutionary naturalism reveal

---

[160] See al-Juwaynī, *al-'Aqīda al-niẓāmiyya*, 38.

[161] See al-Bāqillānī, *al-Tamhīd*, 56; al-Rāzī, *al-Masāil al-khamsūn*, 48.

this dilemma. It is just as paradoxical to think of "creative chance" as to try to imagine a "healthy patient." The deadlocks in the discourse of the evolutionary naturalism can be traced back to this incompatibility. Their solution lies in the clear logic of language. "Creation," as the meaningful coming-to-be of nature, is itself the evidence of a creative will. The question is not whether a creative will exists, but rather, to whom does the creative will belong?

The Qur'an absolutely attributes the creative will, determinant of all nature, to God.[162] As the realization of His will, nature is completely subject to His authority. God is the absolute master of nature; all heaven and earth exhibits His mastery through subjection to His will.[163] In the Qur'an, the Creator is called "*al-malik,*" or "the absolute sovereign."[164] This title signifies the type of authority expressed in the verse:

> *Greatness in the heavens and the earth is rightfully His.*[165]

The Qur'an speaks of the divine majesty as being revealed by the subjection of all creation to the Creator's authority.[166] This submission is described as the "bowing" and "prostration" of creation out of respect for the Creator.[167] All work in the universe belongs to God, all works absolutely return to Him, and the ultimate authority in existence is the creative will of God.[168] With this teaching, the Qur'an rejects any conception of *shirk*, or the assumption that any partners can stand alongside God. The Qur'an proclaims that none of the authorities worshipped with God, none of the nominal deities that are associated with Him, possess anything in the universe, for none of these share His creative will.[169]

> *He does not allow anyone to share His rule.*[170]

[162] See Qur'an 2:22; 7:190; 10:107; 23:117; 29:42; 34:22; 35:40; 39:63; 43:85.
[163] Qur'an 20:6; 67:2.
[164] Qur'an 20:114; 23:116; 59:23.
[165] Qur'an 45:37.
[166] Qur'an 2:116; 30:26.
[167] Qur'an 13:15; 16:49; 22:18.
[168] Qur'an 2:210; 3:154; 11:123; 13:31; 30:4; 42:53.
[169] Qur'an 25:3; 29:17; 34:22; 35:13.
[170] Qur'an 18:26.

This verse metaphorically compares the Creator to a monarch who does not recognize any other ruler in his dominion. In the same way, the heavens and the earth are dedicated to God as the place of his sovereign rule. The universe is compared in the Qur'an to a vast country, and the Creator is this country's absolutely powerful and merciful ruler.[171]

God's domination over nature extends to the natural processes; these are realized according to His divine knowledge. To have mastery over a particular domain, one must know it intimately, and blind domination cannot account for the complex functioning of the natural world. As there can be no mastery without knowledge, nothing that exists in creation can be foreign to the mind of God.[172] In this regard, the Qur'an teaches that God encompasses all of nature in general and all of human life in particular.[173] The entire future is within the dominion of God's rule, and the knowledge of the future pertains to Him.[174] People do not know what will happen to them tomorrow or when and where they will die, but God knows the hidden future.[175] He knows how every human individual will live and how they will cease to live.[176] God knows how the world will end, what will happen on the day of resurrection, how the judged people will respond to God, who will settle in Paradise, and who will be exposed to punishment.[177] In the Qur'an, God's knowledge of everything in the future, as well as in the past, is described by the word "enumeration."[178] This term expresses metaphorically the way in which the divine will specifically determines everything in the universe.

God's determination of the world in all its details is referred to as *al-qadar* in Islamic tradition.[179] In English, this term would correspond

[171] Qur'an 2:107; 3:189; 5:17; 9:116; 24:42.

[172] Cf. al-Ash'arī, *al-Ibāna*, 92; al-Rāzī, *al-Masāil al-khamsūn*, 49; al-Baghdādī, *Uṣūl al-dīn*, 95; al-Taftāzānī, *Sharḥ al-maqāṣid*, II, 95.

[173] Qur'an 3:120; 4:108, 126; 8:47; 11:92; 17:60; 41:54; 65:12.

[174] Qur'an 6:58; 10:20; 11:123; 16:77.

[175] Qur'an 3:179; 6:59; 27:65; 31:34.

[176] Qur'an 47:19.

[177] Qur'an 14:44; 16:86; 19:70; 20:104; 31:43; 34:32; 78:40; 111:3.

[178] Qur'an 36:12; 72:28.

[179] See al-Ṣābūnī, *al-Bidāya*, 78; 'Alī al-Qārī, *Sharḥ Kitāb al-Fiqh al-akbar*, I, 22; al-Birgivī, *Rawḍāt al-jannāt*, 21.

most closely to the idea of "destiny." Meaning literally "measurement" and "determination," God's particular acts of determination, in accordance with His will, are called *taqdīr*.[180] Although the term *qadar* is used in the traditional Muslim language primarily with regard to human life, in a more general sense this term signifies the divine determination of the entire universe. In this sense, *qadar* is directly associated with *tawḥīd*, or faith in the unity of God, which says that there is no creator but God, and that everything comes into being by His will.[181] In Arabic, the original meaning of the verb "to create" (*khalq*) is "to measure out," corresponding to the literal meaning of *qadar*.[182] Therefore, "creation" and "destiny" are two ways of speaking of the same coming-into-being of everything according to a divinely designated measure.[183]

> *Everything has its measure with Him.*[184]
>
> *God has set a due measure for everything.*[185]
>
> *There is not a thing whose storehouses are not with Us. We send it down only by a well-defined measure.*[186]

The intervals of night and day, the regular motions of the sun and the moon, and the phases of development of the human fetus are exemplary manifestations of the divine measure.[187] Rain falls according to a designated determination[188] Food is bestowed upon all creatures according to the divine measure.[189]

Destiny, or *qadar*, is the measure of the creative command. Each command of creation signifies a particular determination, or *taqdīr*.

---

[180] Al-Māturīdī, *al-Tawḥīd*, 307; al-Nasafī, *al-Tamhīd*, 82.

[181] See al-Bayhaqī, *Shu'ab al-īmān*, I, 201; al-Ghaznawī, *Uṣūl al-dīn*, 184; Ibn Taymiyya, *al-Qaḍā wa al-qadar*, 87; Bayāḍīzāda, *al-Uṣūl al-munīfa*, 65.

[182] Al-Zajjāj, *Tafsīr asmā' allāh al-ḥusnā*, 35.

[183] See Qur'an 10:5; 20:40; 25:2; 54:49; 77:22; 80:19.

[184] Qur'an 13:8.

[185] Qur'an 65:3.

[186] Qur'an 15:21.

[187] Qur'an 36:38; 73:20.

[188] Qur'an 23:18; 43:11.

[189] Qur'an 42:27.

The Qur'an teaches that creation exhibits this measure because the divine command itself is measured.[190] Each command is a precisely chosen word through which God creates. In this sense, the divine command is sometimes called the divine "word" in the Qur'an. For example, it is taught repeatedly that God realizes the truth by way of His words.[191] The divine determination of something is called "the passing of the word" (*sabqa al-kalima*).[192] The coming into existence of the determined thing is called "the coming of the command" (*majī al-amr* or *ityān al-amr*), or at times, "the coming true of the word" (*ḥaqq al-kalima* or *ḥaqq al-qawl*).[193] This latter notion is also evident in such language as the "manifestation of the command" (*ẓuhūr al-amr*) and the "execution of the command" (*qaḍā' al-amr*) in the Qur'an.[194] The relationship between the divine command and the word is concisely formulated in the verse of command:

> *When He has ordained something, He only says to it "Be" and it is.*[195]

Moreover, the Qur'an teaches that every command of God is predestined in the divine writing: Whatever is in the world, big or small, living or dead, apparent or hidden, has been written down clearly.[196] There is a script for every destination.[197] Each lifetime is written.[198] Every soul obeys God's will as a term fixed in writing.[199] Nothing befalls a person that God has not written for him.[200] The end of nations is designated and written line by line.[201] In this way, the writing of an entire destiny is the registering of divine sovereignty. Such a transcen-

---

[190] Qur'an 33:38.
[191] Qur'an 2:124; 8:7; 10:82; 42:24.
[192] Qur'an 11:40, 110; 20:129; 41:45.
[193] Qur'an 2:109; 10:24, 33; 11:40, 58; 16:1, 33; 17:16; 28:63; 32:13; 36:70; 39:71; 40:6; 41:25; 46:18.
[194] Qur'an 6:8; 8:42; 9:48; 11:44; 19:21, 39.
[195] Qur'an 3:47; 19:35.
[196] Qur'an 6:59; 11:6; 27:75; 34:3.
[197] Qur'an 13:38.
[198] Qur'an 35:11.
[199] Qur'an 3:145.
[200] Qur'an 9:51.
[201] Qur'an 17:58.

dent knowledge should convince human individuals that divine authority encompasses the whole of their existence. Recognizing this essential limit of their willpower would help them to understand God's demands of servitude, humility, and submission:

> *No misfortune can happen, either in the earth or in yourselves, that was not set down in writing before We bring it into being—that is easy for God—so you need not grieve for what you miss or exult over what He bestows upon you. God does not love the conceited and the boastful.*[202]

Since the divine writing of destiny is transcendent, it cannot be meaningfully compared to any worldly writing. The Qur'an metaphorically refers to the transcendent writing of destiny as a "manifest book" (*kitāb mubīn*) that brings everything in the universe into existence.[203] It is also called the "mother of the book" (*umm al-kitāb*) and "a manifest source" (*imām mubīn*).[204] These attributes equate the transcendent writing of destiny with the divine source of creation. It can even be said that the universe in its strict and necessary accordance to this destiny is a projection of the divinely written book[205]

2. The Wisdom of the Divine Will

Wisdom is simply the knowledge of truth. Wise works are considered true and genuine, whereas unwise works are vain and false. God's supreme wisdom is His knowledge of truth, revealed in His words and actions.[206] The Qur'an states that God works and speaks with absolute wisdom and has no untrue and vain deed.[207] In the Qur'an, God is called *al-Ḥakīm*, "the Perfectly Wise One," because He never wills or acts without truthful purposes.[208] As a divine attribute, *al-Ḥaqq* means

---

[202] Qur'an 57:22, 23.

[203] Qur'an 6:59; 10:61; 11:6; 27:75; 34:3.

[204] Qur'an 13:39; 36:12; 43:4.

[205] Cf. Ragib al-Isfahani, *al-I'tiqadat*, 276.

[206] See al-Zabīdī, *Tāj al-'arūs*, "ḥkm" entry; al-Bayhaqī, *Shu'ab al-īmān*, I, 121; al-Nasafī, *Tabṣira al-adilla*, I, 384.

[207] Qur'an 11:45; 24:18; 30:8; 44:4; 95:8.

[208] Qur'an 2:32, 129, 209; 3:6, 18, 58; 4:26; 16:60; 31:27.

"the True One" or "the Truth."[209] The principle of creation teaches that the meaningful and valuable existence of nature is the result of God's infinitely wise will. Thus the divine Wisdom (that is, His attribute of absolute wisdom) is the source of all meaning and value that we can witness in nature. According to the common argument of classical theologians, the coming into existence of nature in meaningful way testifies absolutely to the wisdom of the Creator. Knowledge is required to bring something so meaningful into existence; in this sense, "creation" necessarily implies "making something wisely." This is why the meaningful existence of nature is proof of the divine wisdom in classical theology.[210] According to such arguments, it is meaningless to speak of the coming into existence of nature without referring to the creative wisdom.

When a person acts unwisely, he or she demonstrates imperfection. Such a fault is incompatible with the concept of the perfection of divinity. The literature of classical theology teaches that God wills according to His absolute wisdom. In other words, the divine will is always consistent with truth.[211] Al-Baghdādī, the Ash'arī theologian of the 11th century, states that the whole Muslim community agrees that God is absolutely wise.[212] But one may come across a hesitation in Ash'arī theology regarding to associate the divine will with absolute wisdom. This hesitation claims that the divine will is not subject to anything and cannot be restricted by any purpose or reason. Historically, this was a protest of "freedom" against the Mu'tazilī theological description of the divine will as "obligated" to justice. The Mu'tazilī discourse of "justice" asserts that God's will is limited to do only what is just and best.[213]

Here the Mu'tazila seem to misunderstand divine justice as a restriction, which led the Ash'arīs to react by insisting that the divine

---

[209] See al-Rāzī, *Lawāmi' al-bayyināt*, 210; al-Zajjājī, *Ishtiqāq asmā' allāh*, 178.

[210] Al-Ash'arī, *al-Luma'*, 24; al-Bāqillānī, *al-Inṣāf*, 53; al-Rāzī, *al-Arba'īn*, I, 188.

[211] Al-Māturīdī, *al-Tawḥīd*, 216; al-Usmandī, *Lubāb al-kalām*, 145; Ibn Taymiyya, *al-Qaḍā wa al-qadar*, 74, 140, 274; Ibn Qayyim al-Jawziyya, *Miftāḥ dār al-sa'āda*, II, 32.

[212] Al-Baghdādī, *al-Farq bayn al-firaq*, 13, 26, 338.

[213] Al-Qāḍī 'Abd al-Jabbār, *al-Mughnī*, VI, 48-49.

will is not bound by any consideration of purpose.[214] In this way, the Ash'arīs unintentionally defamed the divine Wisdom as they tried to affirm the absoluteness of the divine will. But this reactionary picture of divine perfection contradicts the belief of the wider Muslim community, and even the principles of the Ash'arīs' own theology. The Ash'ariyya primarily emphasize God's absolute Wisdom. This is clear as long as Ash'arī theology does not respond to Mu'tazilī theology with such a one-sided formulation.[215]

In the philosophy of nature, the belief in a wisdom that ultimately orders the creation of nature is dealt with in discussions of teleology. Aristotle's category of "purpose" addresses the question "Why is it?" This is one of the four ways in which we can seek the explanation of nature.[216] Here "purpose" refers to the immanent, functional goal of natural structures. For example, a joint in the human body can be explained with reference to its practical purpose: motion and mobility. These functional goals can be objectively determined. Take this statement, for example: "The heart consists of four chambers so that arterial and venous blood will not be mixed." The "so that" here expresses purpose in terms of function. This kind of teleology is widespread in scientific discourse. But physical creatures and structures ultimately demand metaphysical explanations. When asked why a flower exists in the ultimate sense, the answer cannot be determined through an observation of the flower's function. The existential purpose of nature cannot be addressed in the objective discourse of science.[217] To differentiate between these objective and ultimate purposes, some philosophers of biology call the former "teleonomy."[218] It is scientifically "factual" that the eye is for sight and the wing for flight; this is true regardless of all the possible ways that the eye and the

[214] See al-Bāqillānī, *al-Tamhīd*, 50; al-Rāzī, *al-Masāil al-khamsūn*, 62; al-Āmidī, *Ghāya al-marām*, 224.

[215] See al-Bāqillānī, *al-Tamhīd*, 51; al-Ash'arī, *al-Ibāna*, 63-64; al-Isfarāyinī, *al-Tabṣīr*, 168.

[216] Aristotle, *Metaphysics* (tr. Hippocrates G. Apostle), 16.

[217] William J. FitzPatrick, *Teleology and the Norms of Nature*, 179 et seq.

[218] See Jacques Monod, *Chance and Necessity: An Essay on the Natural Philosophy of Modern Biology* (tr. Austryn Wainhouse), 9.

wing may have come into existence. On the other hand, evolutionary naturalists reject any attribution of purpose to nature. They assume that natural structures can exist without recourse to any explanation of intentionality. Many of them even reject teleonomy as the lingering ghost of a medieval metaphysics and choose instead to assert a radical contingency.[219] There is a grain of truth to this approach, for despite its apparent logic, the articulation of objective purposes ultimately has nothing to do with explanation.

The Qur'an seeks to remind its readers of the ultimate telos of nature. The most concise teleological statement in the Qur'an announces that the creation of the world was not without intention:

> *We created the heavens and the earth and all between them not merely in idle sport. We created them only for truth, but most people do not comprehend.*[220]

The world was created "for truth;" this is emphatically repeated in the Qur'an.[221] The Qur'an makes frequent reference to the divine Wisdom with which God created the world and its truths:

> *He is the One Who made the night a garment for you, and sleep a rest, and made the day like a resurrection. He is the One Who sends the winds as heralds of good news before His Mercy. We send down pure water from the sky, so that We can revive a dead land with it, and We give it as a drink to many animals and people We have created.*[222]

The wisdom manifest in creation reveals the Creator's greatness to those who will be mindful.[223] The Qur'an consistently encourages people to see in nature the greatness of God and to contemplate creation as His expression of truth.[224] To seek understanding in this way is to observe the contours of wisdom in creation and recognize the Creator's attributes as they are made manifest:

---

[219] Alan Olding, *Modern Biology and Natural Theology*, 23.
[220] Qur'an 44:38-39.
[221] Qur'an 21:16; 29:44; 30:8; 38:27; 45:22.
[222] Qur'an 25:47-49.
[223] Qur'an 2:164; 3:190; 13:4; 30:28.
[224] Qur'an 3:191; 6:50; 16:69; 30:21.

In His mercy He has made for you night and day, so that you may rest and seek His bounty and be grateful.[225]

Another of His signs is that He sends out the winds bearing good news, giving you a taste of His mercy, that the ships may sail by His command and that you may seek of His bounty, and that you may be grateful.[226]

Here we can see two orders of divine wisdom at work in creation. The first is revealed in the functional design of the world which enables our survival. This includes the creation of night for our rest, oxygen for our breathing, and water for our thirst. This practical design gives form to the fundamental truth of "grace." The other manifestation of divine wisdom relates to the ultimate purpose of the natural world beyond our physical survival, which is the response of and reverence to God that such grace demands. This is the essential truth of "worship." The first order of divine wisdom bestows upon us what we require physically, whereas the second provides a metaphysical explanation for our existence in such a world. The first explains why fruits demonstrate a variety of flavors; the second explains how the person who tastes the fruit should respond to this variety. In this way, the relationship between God and His creatures constitutes the criterion of wisdom present in nature.

As the ultimate purpose of creation, "worship" is simply our response to the unique divinity of the Creator with praise, gratitude, and goodness. In this sense, worship is purely good and the very reason for human existence:

He is the One Who created the heavens and the earth in six Days—His rule extended over the waters—so that He might try you, which of you is best in conduct.[227]

I have created jinn [unseen creatures] and mankind only to serve Me.[228]

He created death and life to try you, which of you is best in conduct.[229]

---

[225] Qur'an 28:73.
[226] Qur'an 30:46.
[227] Qur'an 11:7.
[228] Qur'an 51:56.
[229] Qur'an 67:2.

The Qur'an explains that worship is demanded as the result of divine grace. That is, the created world expresses an unlimited grace that requires a response of worship on the part of humanity. In accordance with this, the Qur'an relates the wisdom of creation to the divine attributes, thereby making the existence of the world a manifestation of the eternal values of divinity.[230] For example, a verse speaking of the creation of diverse blessings for the benefit of humankind ends with the statement: "*For your Lord is kind and merciful.*"[231] It is inferred here that the fundamental reasons for blessings bestowed in the natural world are the divine kindness and mercy. In this manner, the manifest wisdom of creation ultimately expresses the divine attributes, which we must praise in return. In our worship, these attributes are chanted as the divine names. In other words, the eternal values or attributes (such as mercy, kindness, generosity) of the Creator constitute the ultimate wisdom, or reason, of creation. The divine mercy that we praise with the name *Raḥmān* (the Most Merciful One) is the wisdom that orders the boundless manifestations of creation, such as the creation of milk in the mother's breast as the baby is born. The principal truths that God employs in the creation of nature are the eternal values that we express in worship as His names.[232]

Since creation is ultimately rooted in the Creator's eternal values, the existence of nature is absolutely valuable, good, and beautiful in an ultimate sense. No ultimate evil can be attributed to the world, and it is false to speak against nature in this way. Teaching this truth, the Prophet (peace be upon him) forbade accusatory speech towards natural events, animals, and diseases.[233] He rebuked the frustration which falsely assumes that the wind blows unintentionally and worthlessly, admonishing:

> *Do not curse wind; it is by the divine command.*[234]

---

[230] See Qur'an 2:129; 6:13; 22:65; 26:9; 41:2; 57:9; 64:17.

[231] Qur'an 16:7.

[232] Cf. Ibn Qayyim al-Jawziyya, *Miftāḥ dār al-sa'āda*, I, 287.

[233] See Muslim, "Birr," 53; Abū Dāwūd, "Adab," 106; Aḥmad ibn Ḥanbal, V, 193, 299, 311.

[234] Al-Tirmidhī, "Fitan," 65; Ibn Māca, "Adab," 29; Aḥmad ibn Ḥanbal, II, 250, 268.

As nature is absolutely good and beautiful, the Creator deserves love and praise as our response.[235] The absolute praise deserved by God is referred to as *ḥamd* in the Qur'an.[236] God is described as *al-Ḥamīd*, the Praised One.[237] The Qur'an emphasizes that absolute praise should be uniquely offered to God.[238] In fact, this praise of the divine is essentially "worship," the ultimate purpose of human creation.

An important question arises at this point: Why is "worship" the ultimate purpose of our existence and "praise" the ultimate reason for the universe? In effect, this question articulates the teleological problem of "purpose" at the most essential level. In the Islamic metaphysics, an answer to this question would provide the ultimate solution to the problem of "meaning." The question can be answered with reference to the relevant discourses of the Qur'an. In the Qur'an, the Creator Himself praises His sublime Person with great attention and elaboration, revealing His absolute love for His eternal values.[239] Accordingly, He gladly demands of humanity the values that correspond to this divine love, including kindness, justice, patience, trust, prayer, repentance, purity, etc., and forbids ingratitude, unfaithfulness, corruption, injustice, arrogance, and hubris.[240] The Prophet (peace be upon him) also notifies us that God loves beauty, neatness, mildness, and modesty because of His Personal beauty, sanctity, courtesy, and generosity.[241]

In its diverse forms, worship is ultimately the expression of our love for God before His sublime Person and in the presence of His creatures. Our worship then imitates God's own attitude toward His eternal values. It is because God loves and praises His sublime Person that He willed the creation of a universe that would continue to express the praise and love of God that is worship. In this sense, the

---

[235] Cf. Ibn Qayyim al-Jawziyya, *Shifā' al-'alīl*, 595.

[236] Qur'an 1:1; 2:30; 13:13; 15:98; 17:44; 25:58; 27:93; 29:63; 30:18; 31:25.

[237] Qur'an 2:267; 11:73; 14:1; 41:42.

[238] Qur'an 1:1; 6:1; 10:10; 27:59; 28:70; 35:34; 37:182; 40:65; 45:36; 64:1.

[239] See Qur'an 7:54; 23:14; 40:64; 55:78.

[240] See Qur'an 2:190, 195, 222; 3:32, 146, 159; 5:42, 64; 6:141; 16:23.

[241] Al-Bukhārī, "Da'awāt," 69; Muslim "Īmān," 147; "Birr," 77; al-Tirmidhī, "Witr," 2; Abū Dāwūd, "Adab," 130; al-Nasaī, "Ghusl," 7; al-Dārimī, "Riqāq," 75; Mālik, "Isti'dhān," 38; Ahmad ibn Ḥanbal, IV, 133.

existence of nature is ultimately caused by the Creator's love for His own eternal values.[242] To summarize: God respects and loves His infinitely valuable Person in an absolute and transcendent manner, and thus He loves our behavior that conforms to the values of His Personality. The fact that existence ultimately originates in God's transcendent self-respect and self-love has a central emphasis in the literature of Sufism.[243]

God's eternal values comprise the ultimate telos of creation. All wisdom present in creation originates in God's divine values. Let us further examine this truth by returning to the example mentioned above. God's mercy is signified by the divine name *Raḥmān*, and as an enduring characteristic of His divinity, this attribute determines the numerous manifestations throughout creation by way of which the divine mercy is expressed.

> *When those who believe in Our signs come to you, say: Peace be upon you. Your Lord has taken it on Himself to be merciful: if any of you has done a bad deed in ignorance, and afterwards repented and mended his ways, He is most forgiving and most merciful.*[244]

In this verse, mercy is a divine value made manifest in creation from its beginning, and forgiveness can be thought of as yet another expression of this mercy. At a subsequent level, forgiveness has its origin in this eternal attribute of mercy. If we trace the lines of this conceptual unfolding, we see mercy expand into countless manifestations in nature. For example, the divine acceptance of prayer and response to our needs, the provision of food and patience, guidance towards truth and slowness to anger, all of these expressions of mercy originate in the fundamental divine attribute.[245] To continue, the divine quality of "guiding to truth" structures the proliferation of subsequent expressions of mercy, included the sending of prophets, bestowing of revelations, reminding of the truths, and so on. Furthermore, the "sending of prophets" gives rise to other expressions of divine mercy: supporting

---

[242] Cf. Ibn Qayyim al-Jawziyya, *Shifā' al-'alīl*, 49.

[243] See Ibn Qayyim al-Jawziyya, *Shifā' al-'alīl*, 542, 593.

[244] Qur'an 6:54.

[245] See Qur'an 2:186, 218, 225; 6:142; 20:50; 22:60.

the prophets, giving them good news regarding their mission, protecting them from enemies, etc.[246]

This unfolding of the eternal values of divinity in creation is described in the Qur'an as the "elaboration of the signs" (*tafṣīl al-āyāt*).[247] As mentioned above, these "signs" are the qualities of creation that ultimately testify to the manifestation of divine names.

> *We made the night and day as two signs. We darkened the night and made the daylight for seeing, that you may seek bounty from your Lord and that you may know how to count the years and calculate. We have elaborated everything perfectly.*[248]

It can be said that every moment of existence is a manifestation of divine wisdom.[249] For instance, when I see a cherry tree, I see the manifest values of organization, justice, and artistry revealed in the build of the tree and the efficiency of its photosynthesis. Goodness, purity, and gentleness, are revealed in the delicate blossoms that embellish its branches, and mercy, compassion, and generosity are revealed in the nectar that is given to insects and the cherries bestowed upon people, and so on. If these manifest values are expressed in relation to their corresponding divine names, then "remembrance" (*dhikr*) is realized. Namely, God is remembered, loved, and praised through our utterance of the relevant divine names: *Raḥmān*, most merciful, *Raḥīm*, most compassionate, *Khāliq*, creator, *Ṣāni'*, artist, *'Ādil*, just, *Jamīl*, beautiful, *Muḥsin*, gracious, *Quddūs*, most pure, *Razzāq*, provider, *Karīm*, bountiful, and so forth. In fact, these names find their very first expression in the creation of the tree. Thus the cherry tree itself expresses the glory of its Creator, and in a sense celebrates God's divine attributes. Creation's necessary expression of the divine glory is called *tasbīḥ* in the Qur'an, meaning "exaltation." Every creature naturally and inevitably exalts God by making His values manifest.[250] This endless and perpetual exaltation is the sacred language of nature,

---

[246] See Qur'an 2:213; 5:67; 14:4; 27:93; 40:51.

[247] Qur'an 6:98; 10:5; 13:2.

[248] Qur'an 17:12.

[249] Cf. Ibn Qayyim al-Jawziyya, *Shifā' al-'alīl*, II, 32.

[250] Qur'an 17:44; 24:41; 57:1; 59:1.

revealing the ultimate purpose of existence.[251] This is the point where the purpose of nature and the purpose of the Book coincide. Namely, nature teaches the divine names just as the Qur'an does:

> *He is God: there is no god other than Him, the One who knows what is hidden and what is in the open. He is most gracious, most merciful. He is God: there is no god other than Him, the Sovereign, the Holy One, the Source of Peace, the Granter of Security, the Guardian, the Almighty, the Compeller, the Great. God is far above any partners they attribute to Him. He is God, the Creator, the Originator, the Shaper. To Him belong the best names. Everything in the heavens and earth glorifies Him. He is the Almighty, the Wise.*[252]

The elaborate manifestations of divine wisdom revealed in the creation of nature, the particular design of the hand for our convenience for example, are ensue from the eternal values of divinity. Given the notion of "elaboration" mentioned above, the divine attributes revealed in creation should not be considered apart from the creation in which they are revealed. In this regard, the eternal values of divinity are primary and absolute while their elaborate manifestations in creation are secondary. The Qur'an gives examples of such manifestations:

> *God has written, "I shall most certainly win, I and My messengers." God is powerful and almighty.*[253]

> *Our word has been passed for Our servants the messengers: it is they who will be helped.*[254]

These verses and others like them indicate that divine wisdom is determined and registered by divine words. The divine words of wisdom, like those of destiny, are written in a transcendent sense.[255] This is what the Prophet (peace be upon him) means when he says that the superiority of God's mercy over His wrath was written at the begin-

---

[251] Cf. Seyyed Hossein Nasr, *Religion and the Order of Nature*, 289.
[252] Qur'an 59:22-24.
[253] Qur'an 58:21.
[254] Qur'an 37:171-172.
[255] See Qur'an 5:32, 45; 6:12, 54; 7:156; 21:105; 59:3.

ning of creation.[256] In the Qur'an, the transcendent writing of the divine words is called the "mother of the book," "a manifest book," and "a manifest source."[257] The written record of destiny in the transcendent book of God registers the divine sovereignty. The written record of divine Wisdom, however, registers God's purposes that inform this sovereignty. The transcendent writing of divine Wisdom constitutes the limits and ends of creation and precedes the writing of destiny. Destiny is written within the boundaries established by the writing of divine Wisdom, in which the Master of the universe always wills the truth.[258] The written record of Wisdom can also be called the code of divine morality, for it reveals the norms according to which God behaves. The Qur'an refers to the divine morality with the word *sunnatullāh*, literally "God's way."[259] The Qur'an emphasizes that God's way never changes because His words of wisdom are definite and complete.[260]

3. The Perpetual Rule of the Divine Will

The fact that God determines all of nature according to His wisdom means that His will is perpetually active. The ongoing existence of nature depends upon the ongoing authority of the divine will. In other words, nature comes into being only for as long as God wills it. In this way, existence rests absolutely upon God's constant act of willing. The Qur'an calls God *al-Ṣamad*, the One who is self-sufficient and satisfies the needs of others.[261] This attribute indicates that God is absolutely independent of creatures, but creatures are in absolute need of God. The universe's need for God is directly apparent in the definition of "creation": God's creative will comes prior to the resultant universe, and the Creator precedes all of His creatures.[262] The Qur'an refers to

[256] Al-Bukhārī, "Tawḥīd," 55; "Bad' al-khalq," 1; Muslim, "Tawba," 14; Ibn Māca, "Zuhd," 35.
[257] Qur'an 6:59; 10:61; 11:6; 13:39; 27:75; 34:3; 36:12; 43:4.
[258] See 'Abd al-Karīm Zaydān, *al-Sunan al-ilāhiyya*, 23.
[259] Qur'an 33:38; 40:85; 48:23.
[260] Qur'an 6:34, 115; 7:137; 10:64; 33:62; 35:43; 48:23.
[261] Qur'an 112:2.
[262] Al-Bācūrī, *Tuḥfa al-murīd*, 47.

God's absolute priority with the attribute *al-Awwal*, or "the One who is the first."[263] This absolute priority necessarily implies "eternality," since the former is the state of absolute originality that admits of no beginning in its infinity.[264] As the Qur'an states, God is sole, unique, and not generated.[265] The existence and life of God are the only eternal existence and life. In the Qur'an, God is called both *al-Ḥayy*, the One who is alive and immortal, and *al-Qayyūm*, the One who is perpetual and the source of perpetuity.[266] Since God is uniquely eternal, He does not owe His existence and life to anything, for He bestows existence and life upon everything. It is worth noting that the name *al-Qayyūm* is derived from a verb that is both transitive and intransitive. Thus it can refer simultaneously to both the infinity of the divine Person and to His bestowal of existence upon the universe.[267]

Is it possible to understand "infinity" as the eternality of the divine Person? Needless to say, the answer lies in a precise definition of "infinity." The everyday understanding of infinity, which should not be overlooked, describes a limitlessness of a value such as number or time.[268] This simply means that, for any imaginable quantity, it is always possible to imagine a point just beyond the present totality, hence there is always the possibility that the totality could be expanded infinitely. For us, the meaning of infinity is nothing but this possibility.[269] Although as humans we cannot observe any infinite value, it would not be meaningful to doubt the possibility of infinity where a limit is not logically allowed.[270] In the previous section, I suggested that it is impossible to define the limits of the ultimate reality because the whole of existence depends on it. God's infinity can be conceived of only as His absolute precedence to creation. This is how the divine name *al-Aww-*

[263] Qur'an 57:3.

[264] Ibn Fūrak, *Mujarrad maqālāt al-Shaykh*, 43.

[265] Qur'an 112:1, 3.

[266] Qur'an 2:255; 3:2; 20:111.

[267] Al-Zajjāj, *Tafsīr asmā' allāh al-ḥusnā*, 56; al-Isfarāyinī, *al-Tabṣīr*, 156.

[268] Rene Guenon, *The Multiple States of the Being*, 7.

[269] See Rudy Rucker, *Infinity and the Mind*, 37.

[270] Cf. Descartes, *Principles of Philosophy* (tr. Valentine Rodger Miller and Reese P. Miller), 13.

al, "the First," must be read. Such a conception of the divine infinity also finds its expression in the words of the Prophet: "There was God and nothing with Him."[271] God's infinite life remains unknown to us until He himself offers to speak of it. In this regard, God's transcendent life is both the ultimate truth and the ultimate mystery, what the Sufi tradition calls "the truth of the truths" (*ḥaqīqa al-ḥaqāiq*) and "the essential curtain" (*'ayn al-barzakh*). These formulations of the divine infinity suggest that God's life is eternally for Himself, and as al-Ghazzālī says, the curtain is only for us, the created ones.[272]

The Creator's perpetual willing activity directly indicates His vitality, for action is the evidence of life.[273] As the Qur'an eloquently puts it: "*He is always engaged upon a matter.*"[274] The divine engagement is also expressed in the verse: "*Neither slumber nor sleep overtakes Him.*"[275] The divine life is perfect then, for the divine will does not cease to be active.[276] With regard to the principle of creation, the clearest evidence of this constancy is the continual creation of nature in its boundless abundance. The ongoing creation we witness in nature indicates not only the perpetual rule of the divine will, but also the perpetuity of the divine life. The divine names *al-Ḥayy* and *al-Qayyūm* are thus elucidated beautifully in the very fact of nature's existence. This elucidation also reveals the ultimate meaning of time. That is, "time" refers to nothing but this "continuity of existence," which expresses the perpetual rule of the divine will. In other words, what we call the progression of time is ultimately characterized by the continuity of creation. Time reveals the continual effect of the divine command, which testifies to the perpetual rule of the divine will, which characterizes the perpetual life of the Creator. Therefore, the ultimate meaning of time relates to the divine life. In this respect, the Prophet

[271] Al-Bukhārī, "Tawḥīd," 22; "Bad' al-khalq," 1.
[272] Cf. al-Ghazzālī, *Mishkāt al-anwār*, 47.
[273] Cf. Al-Āmidī, *al-Mubīn*, 102.
[274] Qur'an 55:29.
[275] Qur'an 2:255.
[276] Al-Ghazzālī, *Ma'ārij al-quds*, 164.

(peace be upon him) forbade speaking against time, for time relates ultimately to the divinity.[277]

In the principle of creation, it is clear that the divine life is the very origin of time. But strangely enough, the relation between time and divinity has remained one of the most intricate problems of theology. The problem can be concisely expressed by the question: "What does time mean about God?" The famous answer of all major metaphysical positions in the Islamic tradition is that time does not mean anything about God.[278] This answer, intending to assert God's "transcendence over time," actually disrupts the clear logic of creation. From this negative answer, it is impossible to articulate the infinity of divine life, the perpetual rule of the divine will, and the continual effect of the divine command. The confusion begins with a pseudo-definition of eternity. Traditional literatures assert that the eternality of God does not mean infinity in time. Instead, it must mean "timelessness," an alleged state that transcends all of the limitations of time. But with this pseudo-definition at the foundation of traditional theology, the divine names *al-Ḥayy* and *al-Qayyūm* lose their real meaning. Subsequently, all other divine attributes becomes obscure: there can no longer be such a thing as the perpetual rule of the divine will, or the continual effect of the divine command. God's continuous loving, showing mercy, seeing, hearing, and speaking, all collapse into ambiguity.

The exaltation of divinity from time is consistent with the tradition of Platonic philosophy. In this tradition, time is associated with change, while perfection must always be "immutable" and "timeless." In his renowned dialog on the creation of the world, Plato writes that time pertains to nature and the divine life is exalted above this temporal realm.[279] Plato's anti-time metaphysic was inherited by Neo-Platonic philosophy and influenced a wide variety of thinkers. Plotinus of Alexandria, 3rd century CE, argued that eternity and time are in contra-

---

[277] Al-Bukhārī, "Tawḥīd," 53; Abū Dāwūd, "Adab," 169; Aḥmad ibn Ḥanbal, V, 299, 311.

[278] See Al-Ghazzālī, *Ma'ārij al-quds*, 172; al-Ījī, *al-Mawāqif*, 275; al-Fārābī, *al-Ta'līqāt*, 372; Ibn Sīnā, *al-Ilāhiyyāt*, 185, 373; Ibn Rushd, *Tahāfut al-Tahāfut*, 65; Ibn 'Arabī, *al-Futūḥāt al-Makkiyya*, I, 198; al-Jīlī, *al-Insān al-kāmil*, 31, 60.

[279] Plato, *Timaeus* (tr. Benjamin Jowett), 20.

diction, and that God's infinity can only be expressed as timelessness.[280] The anti-time metaphysic of Muslim philosophers originates in this Platonic speculation.[281] However, the origin of the anti-time discourse in classical Islamic theology seems to be independent of that influence and grounded in a different speculation. The speculative deduction of the proof of the temporality of the universe, thus its creation, has come to be known as the argument of *ḥudūth*, literally meaning "occurrence." Originally formulated by some rationalist theologians in the early 8th century, this argument is widely known in virtually all theological schools. The argument concludes that every occurrence in the universe indicates that it is not eternal and must have come into existence by the will of an eternal creator. Here is a simplified version of the deduction:

> (a) The universe essentially consists of substances, which are subject to temporal states.
> (b) Nothing in a temporal state can be permanent.
> (c) Therefore, the universe is not eternal, but must have had a beginning.[282]

It is ironic that this most celebrated syllogism in the literature of the classical theology is flawed. Temporal states in the universe, such as those relating to motion and form, do not necessarily prove the impermanence of anything. There is no logical necessity that can equate contingency with the disappearance of substance. In the simplest terms, death is the end of life but not its consequence. A human person, if preserved from the physical degeneration of the body, can live forever. In terms of physics, a mass in motion does not disappear as long as its substance is preserved. For this reason, the argument from *ḥudūth* is not able to respond to the fundamental objection of the Aristotelian naturalism: Why can we not suppose that the universe exists eternally according to its necessary substance? This argument also neglects the major questions of how eternal life can be considered within the domain of the argument of *ḥudūth,* and how this theology

[280] Plotinus, *The Enneads* (tr. Stephen MacKenna), 62, 253.
[281] See Majid Fakhry, *A History of Islamic Philosophy*, 19 et seq.
[282] See al-Bāqillānī, *Tamhīd*, 44; al-Nasafī, *Tabṣira al-adilla*, I, 44 et seq.

can account for the temporal states of Paradise without denying its permanence. It seems that the classical theology does not carefully investigate the structure of the argument. Without any doubts regarding its validity, all of the argument's logical consequences were theologically advocated. Remarkably, classical theologians made every experience a proof of the temporal nature of existence, even a single act, considering such experiences to be at odds with the permanence of the eternal.[283]

The argument of *ḥudūth* does not prove the temporality of the universe; it is simply a false syllogism. Worse, the argument encourages an anti-time metaphysics similar to the Platonic philosophy by emphasizing a contradiction between time and eternity. The literature of classical theology begins with the argument of *ḥudūth,* and its subsequent deductions are flawed accordingly. Now this false logic has been mistakenly established as a foundation for theology. Al-Māturīdī writes: "We cannot consider these marks of temporality to relate to God, since it is these marks that prove the temporality of the universe."[284] The marks al-Māturīdī refers are all those that designate the temporality of experience, relating to the linearity of the past, present, and future rather than the transcendence of eternity. He is concerned that if temporality is attributed to God in any way, the divine eternality can no longer be proven. This confusion typifies the very defect of the argument of *ḥudūth.* God is supposedly exalted above everything that is associated with time. This principle of absolute transcendence is referred to as God's "dissimilarity to temporal things" (*al-mukhālafa li al-ḥawādith*). The consequences of this principle for divine action can be summarized as follows: God is exalted from any temporal states. Thus the divine acts are not subject to temporality and do not relate to time. Past, present and future are not true for God; His attributes are eternal. His will is eternally a single act that transcends time.[285]

---

[283] See al-Rāzī, *al-Masāil al-khamsūn*, 19.

[284] Al-Māturīdī, *al-Tawḥīd*, 69.

[285] See al-Māturīdī, *al-Tawḥīd*, 69; al-Nasafī, *Tabṣira al-adilla*, I, 110; al-Juwaynī, *Luma'u al-adilla*, 109; al-Usmandī, *Lubāb al-kalām*, 75; al-Ījī, *al-Mawāqif*, 274; al-Taftāzānī, *Sharḥ al-'Aqāid*, 111; al-Bayḍāwī, *Ṭawāli' al-anwār*, 171, 172.

The perpetual rule of the divine will cannot be articulated within this discourse of *ḥudūth*, for the attribute of "willing" can only be instantiated in singular acts of the will. It is meaningless to say that God's will is "eternally a single act," for this signifies nothing about God's perpetual sovereignty over the universe. The question to ask is this: Can any act be attributed to eternity? God's speaking, seeing, hearing, willing, commanding, loving, showing mercy, having pleasure or discontent, etc. are "eternal" insofar as they are unmaterialized attributes, but His particular acts of willing something, saying something, commanding something, seeing something, hearing something, loving someone, having mercy upon somebody, etc. can by no means be attributed to eternity. For instance, God's forgiveness occurs in a necessary sequence: after a person asks for repentance. And only as a consequence of this forgiveness can God's love and pleasure replace the discontent. Here the temporality of the sequence is extremely important.

The discourse of *ḥudūth* plunges theology interminably into the problem of time. In the early centuries of Islamic theology, the solution to this problem would have been to re-examine the premises of the original argument, but theologians moved forward. Sunnī theologians provided an *ad hoc* speculation called *ta'alluq* (relevance). In this proposed resolution, divine acts are eternally single although they may "relate" to temporal states over the course of creation.[286] For instance, God's eternal will is a single act that relates uniquely to every occurrence in the universe; this is how He can rule over the plurality of existence without being dirtied by any relation to temporality.[287] Needless to say, *ta'alluq* is a paltry term fabricated to relate the so-called "timeless" divine act with temporal existence that ignores the absurdity inherent in the concept of an "eternally single act." This does nothing but introduce more irrationality into the discourse of *ḥudūth*. Historically, Sunnī theologians have been uncomfortable with this explanation of *ta'alluq*, but they held to it so as not to upset the

[286] See al-Baghdādī, *Uṣūl al-dīn*, 102; al-Ghazzālī, *Iḥyā' 'ulūm al-dīn*, I, 149.

[287] See Ibn Fūrak, *Mujarrad maqālāt al-Shaykh*, 69; al-Rāzī, *al-Arba'īn*, I, 246; al-Shahristānī, *Nihāya al-aqdām*, 238; al-Bayḍāwī, *Ṭawāli' al-anwār*, 187; al-Farrā, *al-Mu'tamad fī uṣūl al-dīn*, 73.

argument of *ḥudūth*. In the face of any objections, this Sunnī position can only repeat the affirmation that no temporal states can be attributed to God's eternal Person.[288] Muʿtazilī theologians, on the other hand, tended to admit the temporality of the particular divine acts while still defending the argument of *ḥudūth*. This led to the invention of a number of new speculations in an attempt to reconcile this contradiction. The Muʿtazilīs of Baghdad dared to suggest that divine acts, including God's actions of seeing and hearing, were "figurative," denying them any temporal meaning.[289] Other Muʿtazilīs chose to accept the real meaning of the divine acts but peculiarly claimed that they do not belong to God's Person.[290]

There is another discourse, marginal compared to the previous speculations, that moves past the argument of *ḥudūth*. Here "eternity" regains its proper denotation, clearly referring to infinity.[291] In this tradition, the divine existence and life are defined according to their perpetuity, and the names *al-Ḥayy* and *al-Qayyūm* recover their original meaning.[292] The divine acts are understood to be temporal states, whereas the divine attributes relating to those acts are eternal. In other words, a particular divine act occurs in temporality as a manifestation of the eternal character of the divine Person. God is eternally the Creator, or "one who is always able to create," even though He only creates certain things at certain times. Theologians explain this relationship through several examples from daily life: "a scribe is always a scribe, even when not writing," or "a tailor is always a tailor, even when not sewing."[293] In his non-speculative work on divine attributes, al-Ghazzālī, states that God is eternally the Almighty even if He has not yet ordered for the creation of *Qiyāma*, the Resurrection.[294] Al-Rāzī, in his non-dialectical work on divine attributes, writes:

---

[288] See al-Ghazzālī, *al-Iqtiṣād*, 159; al-Subkī, *al-Sayf al-mashhūr*, 14.

[289] See al-Ashʿarī, *Maqālāt al-Islāmiyyīn*, I, 235, 256; al-Qāḍī ʿAbd al-Jabbār, *al-Mughnī*, V, 241.

[290] See al-Qāḍī ʿAbd al-Jabbār, *Sharḥ al-Uṣūl al-khamsa*, 168, 174, 440, 535.

[291] See al-Rāzī, *al-Arbaʿīn*, I, 308.

[292] See al-Rāzī, *Lawāmiʿ al-bayyināt*, 207, 257.

[293] See al-Māturīdī, *al-Tawḥīd*, 47; al-Nasafī, *Baḥr al-kalām*, 9, 38; al-Ghazzālī, *al-Iqtisād*, 104, 158; al-Subkī, *al-Sayf al-mashhūr*, 14.

[294] Al-Ghazzālī, *al-Maqṣad al-asnā*, 145.

> God is all-hearing. If you run into difficulty, He responds to your prayer. When you are helpless, He surmounts your trouble. When you repent, He forgives your fault. When you apologize, He accepts your apology. He has mercy upon you in the time of weakness and sadness.[295]

Here is a theological discourse rooted in common sense. Historians note that this position was ardently defended by the small sect called al-Karrāmiyya, a marginal group condemned by the Sunnī theologians as heretical for their anthropomorphism.[296] The late Salafī school of theology also exhibited a comparable understanding, admitting that temporal acts of creation demonstrate the perfection of the divine life.[297] The relevant Sufi discourse is similar: God is infinitely active generating perpetual manifestations.[298] But in the environment of broad philosophical speculation inspired by the argument of *ḥudūth*, classical theologians typically abandoned these simple formulations.[299]

The anti-time metaphysic, though questionable, has found a place in all of the major traditions. The classical Ash'arī theologian al-Ījī remarks that all people of religion and philosophy agree that God must transcend time in order to be truly eternal.[300] It is possible to see in this "agreement" the customary game that speculative philosophy plays against the logic of everyday experience. Simple logic prevails in the language of daily life, even in the language of theology, but once time is contemplated speculatively, the game begins. Two aspects particular to the Islamic metaphysical tradition encourage this sort of speculation. The first is the failure to realize the invalidity of the argument of *ḥudūth* as outlined above. The second is the obligation of adherence, conscious or not, to Platonic assumptions. Both attempt to exalt the eternal above the realm of perpetual activity. To bring this

---

[295] Al-Rāzī, *Lawāmi' al-bayyināt*, 180.

[296] See al-Rāzī, *I'tiqādāt*, 67; al-Baghdādī, *al-Farq bayn al-firaq*, 219.

[297] See Ibn Taymiyya, *al-Asmā' wa al-ṣifāt*, 461; Ibn Qayyim al-Jawziyya, *Shifā' al-'alīl*, 526.

[298] See al-Jīlī, *al-Insān al-kāmil*, 63.

[299] See al-Rāzī, *al-Arba'īn*, I, 168.

[300] Al-Ījī, *al-Mawāqif*, 274.

speculative game to an end, Islamic metaphysics must reject flawed logic and take seriously the language of the Qur'an. This makes it possible to speak about the meaning of time in respect to the divine existence and opens our ears to the Prophet's wisdom that understands time as an essential feature of the divine life. We must return to the original sense of infinity when we read in the Qur'an that "*a day near God is like a thousand years for people.*"[301]

Time, signifying the continuity of existence, is ultimately evidence of the perpetual rule of the divine will. This is the essence of the principle of creation. As stated above, the divine will can only be "perfect" if it is perpetual, and it can only be "eternal" if it continues forever. Therefore time, with regard to the divinity, demonstrates the permanence of the creative will and the eternality of the divine life. This permanence and perpetuity is exactly what is meant by the divine names *al-Ḥayy* and *al-Qayyūm*. In his exceptional analysis, al-Rāzī defines time as the "quality of being" (*kawn*) for everything that exists, including the divine Person.[302] Abū al-Barakāt al-Baghdādī, the great 12th century philosopher, defines the progression of time in terms of the "continuity of existence" and interprets the divine infinity as expressing the absolute perpetuity of the divine existence and life.[303] These definitions, grounded in the logic of the experience of being, put a halt to philosophical speculation that announces time to be a "mystery" begging to be solved. On the contrary, if the concept of "time" cannot be explained, it is only because it is so simple and evident. It is just the same with the concept of "existence."[304] The experience of "existence" remains constant despite all relative perceptions of time. This latter fact makes all discussions of "timelessness" into vanity that speaks of nothing.[305] From this vantage, the attempt to solve the so-called mystery of time is destined to failure. Saint Augustine's words exemplify this impasse:

---

301 Qur'an 22:47.

302 Al-Rāzī, *al-Mabāhith al-mashriqiyya*, I, 581.

303 Abū al-Barakāt al-Baghdādī, *al-Mu'tabar*, III, 39-41.

304 Cf. Thomas Sattig, *The Language and Reality of Time*, 58.

305 Cf. Errol E. Harris, *The Reality of Time*, 51.

> What is time? Who can explain this easily and briefly? Who can comprehend this even in thought so as to articulate the answer in words? Yet what do we speak of, in our familiar everyday conversation, more than of time? We surely know what we mean when we speak of it. We also know what is meant when we hear someone else talking about it. What then is time? Provided that no one asks me, I know. If I want to explain it to an inquirer, I do not know.[306]

He might as well have said: "Existence is so explicit that I cannot explain it." Such explanation is not possible, just as it is impossible to explain God's perpetual creativity from within the boundaries of Platonic philosophy or the argument of *ḥudūth*.

[306] Augustine, *Confessions* (tr. Henry Chadwick), 230.

II.

God's Creative Speech

1. The Power of the Divine Speech

According to the principle of creation, the divine command is the source of the nature's realization. In other words, the result of the divine command is the display of divine power. All creation depends on this ultimate source: God's creative command as a mode of His speech.[307] This is indicated by the verse of command in the Qur'an:

> *When We will something to happen, all that We say is, "Be," and it is.*[308]

God's speech is His creative power. In this regard, Ibn 'Arabī, the great Sufi philosopher of the 13th century, equates divine speech with divine power.[309] As I will elaborate later, the principle of creation implies that all forces effective in the process of nature are the manifestation of the power of the divine command. It is therefore necessary to make the divine command equivalent to the work that it accomplishes in the universe. This is displayed in the Arabic word *amr*. The word has two primary meanings: "command," or "order," and "work," or "matter." In the first case, the plural is *awāmir* (commands, orders), and in the second, *umūr* (works, matters).[310] The nuance of this double meaning

---

[307] See al-Sarakhsī, *Uṣūl*, I, 11, 13.

[308] Qur'an 16:40.

[309] Cağfer Karadaş, *Ibn Arabi'nin İtikadi Görüşleri*, 114.

[310] See Ibn Manẓūr, *Lisān al-'Arab*, "amr" entry.

opens up the verse of command to its dynamic interpretation. For example, consider this version of the verse: "*When He decrees an 'amr', He says only, 'Be,' and it is.*"[311] The first part of the sentence can be rendered both: "decrees a command" and "decrees a matter."[312] Namely, God's transcendent utterance of a command for the creation of a matter is equivalent to the coming-into-being of that matter.

God realizes His will through His command. It is carried out, operated, and implemented in the universe through His divine speech. This means that the divine act of creation is identical to the divine act of imperative speech.[313] Indeed, the absolute authority of divine power depends on this identity. For God, the act of creation requires nothing more than the expression of a command. Therefore the efficacy of creative power solely rests upon the content of the command. The power of the divine command is its imperative meaning. In other words, when God has commanded the occurrence of anything, He has already exerted the power effective for the realization of the occurrence. God can command whatever He wills; there is no hindrance to His imperative. It is this freedom that makes the divine power absolute. In the realm of humanity, however, the relationship between will and power is inverted. Human will is limited by human power, for one can will only in proportion to one's power. Here "will" must be distinguished from "wish" or "desire." One can wish for the coming spring, for instance, but cannot will it. By contrast, in the Creator, will is the source of power, and thus His power is in proportion to His will: it is absolute. In God, power is limited only by will, whereas, in creatures, will is limited by power.

In order to explain the absolute authority of the divine power, the Qur'an often makes comparisons to domains of human authority. For example, the Qur'an compares the divine, creative command to the single act of an eye blinking. In the figurative sense, a powerful ruler is one who can implement his will with the mere raising of his hand.[314] Likewise, in order to emphasize God's power over the remaking of the

---

[311] Qur'an 2:117; 3:47; 40:68.

[312] See Abū al-Su'ūd, *Irshād al-'aql al-salīm*, I, 151.

[313] Cf. al-Bayhaqī, *al-Asmā' wa al-ṣifāt*, 138; al-Ghazzālī, *Ma'ārij al-quds*, 172.

[314] Qur'an 54:50.

world in the Hereafter, the Qur'an says figuratively that God was not wearied by the creation of the heavens and the earth.[315] Prophet Abraham (peace be upon him) prays to God asking to be shown him how God will resurrect the dead. God responds:

> *Take four birds and train them to come back to you. Then place them on separate hilltops, call them back, and they will come flying to you. Then know that God is all powerful and wise.*[316]

This verse teaches that the resurrection of the dead will be accomplished through a single divine command—a single call.[317] The Qur'an states that God's command is absolutely effectual; there can be no resistance to it, for it always comes true.[318] The Qur'an consistently teaches that God has power over all things.[319] God does absolutely whatever He wills, for power belongs exclusively to Him.[320] There is no power independent of the divine power, and nothing can incapacitate the Creator.[321]

> *To God belongs the sovereignty of the heavens and earth and all that is between them. He creates whatever He will. God has power over everything.*[322]

> *God created each animal out of a fluid. Some of them crawl on their bellies, some walk on two legs, and some on four. God creates whatever He will. God has power over everything.*[323]

The power exhibited by the divine speech can be compared to a phenomenon in linguistics called "perlocutionary speech acts." Certain words can influence their hearers directly. For example, yelling

---

[315] Qur'an 46:33; 50:15.

[316] Qur'an 2:260.

[317] See al-Rāzī, *al-Tafsīr al-kabīr*, VII, 37.

[318] Qur'an 4:47; 8:42; 12:21; 13:41; 33:37; 65:3.

[319] Qur'an 2:20, 106, 109; 3:29, 165; 5:19, 40; 8:41; 9:39; 16:77; 29:20; 35:1; 59:6.

[320] Qur'an 2:253; 3:40; 11:107; 14:27; 22:14; 85:16.

[321] Qur'an 2:165; 18:39; 29:22; 35:44.

[322] Qur'an 5:17.

[323] Qur'an 24:45.

"Watch out!" directly causes the hearer to take action; the speaker directly exhibits force through speech.[324] All words that cause such effect can be considered as perlocutionary speech acts: from a commander's "Quick march!" to a lover's "I love you" to a father's encouragement to his son, "You'll succeed!" Indeed, speech is power. To draw an allegory from this linguistic notion, God's creative command is the manifestation of His speech that dominates the field towards which it is directed. The divine command is directed towards the whole of nature, and thus dominates the universal space in which all physical forces and entities come into existence. For instance, the divine command that orders the creation of the sky ultimately regulates all natural functions that pertain to precipitation. So rain is created as well. In the same way, the movement of a sailboat is ultimately governed by the interplay of natural factors that are the result of the divine command:

> *Another of His signs is that He sends out the winds bearing good news, giving you a taste of His mercy, that the ships may sail by His command and that you may seek of His bounty, and that you may be grateful.*[325]

The fact that divine power is a feature of divine speech is often neglected in the literature of classical theology, which obscured the vivid and vital relation of God's speech to His creative power and made the divine act of creation into something ambiguous and indefinite. The main reason for such neglect was discussed above: the argument of *ḥudūth*. According to this argument, the divine act of imperative speech can have no relation to the domain of time. The discourse of *ḥudūth* is an absolute obstacle to understanding the fact that "divine speech" means God's act of "speaking," just as "divine will" means His act of "willing." In classical theological literature, the divine speech is defined as "eternally a single attribute" with emphasis on its non-temporality.[326] Al-Rāzī observes a consensus among Sunnī Muslims regard-

---

[324] See François Recanati, *Meaning and Force*, 10.

[325] Qur'an 30:46.

[326] See al-Nasafī, *Tabṣira al-adilla*, I, 259, 306; Ibn Fūrak, *Mujarrad maqālāt al-shaykh*, 59; al-Juwaynī, *Luma' al-adilla*, 102; al-Isfarāyinī, *al-Tabṣīr*, 167;

ing the eternality of the divine speech.[327] A common confession in Sunnī theology is that God's speech is eternal; the divine word is not created.[328] The problem, as discussed above, is that the very act of speaking (of creating words) cannot be attributed to eternity, although the capacity for speech (as possibility) can. How can anything "be said" in eternity? What does it mean to say that a divine word, such as a sentence from the Qur'an or a command of creation, is spoken by God in eternity?

This problem can only be solved by appealing to the logic of our common-sense experience of time. Otherwise, the problem is exaggerated in the discourse of *ḥudūth*. As we have seen, theologians ultimately found no other way to reconcile the divine acts with the divine eternality than by creating speculative categories such as "timelessness" or "relevance." It is a standard affirmation of Sunnī theology that the divine speech is a single eternal attribute that relates to an unlimited number of divine words throughout creation.[329] On the other hand, the Mu'tazilī theologians considered it meaningless to attribute eternality to a spoken word. Thus they argued that the Qur'an, which consists of the divine words spoken by God as revelation, are not eternal but temporal. In articulating this argument, these theologians often used the word "created" (*makhlūq*) to describe the Qur'an.[330] By this they meant "temporally made" (*muḥdath*).[331] Against al-Mu'tazila, Sunnī theologians thought this designation of the Qur'an as something created was an "illegitimate innovation" (*bid'a*), and they justified their opposition with reference to the argument of *ḥudūth*. They even announced it a "heresy" to think that God's creative command, His act of imperative speech, could be temporal.[332] In this way, the relationship between power and the divine speech was obscured in the history of Islamic theology.

---

al-Ghaznawī, *Uṣūl al-dīn*, 102; al-Lāmishī, *al-Tamhīd*, 71.

[327] Al-Rāzī, *Ma'ālim uṣūl al-dīn*, 50.

[328] Ibn Qudāma, *al-I'tiqād*, 33; al-Farrā, *al-Mu'tamad*, 86.

[329] Al-Shahristānī, *Nihāya al-aqdām*, 288; al-Ghaznawī, *Uṣūl al-dīn*, 105.

[330] Al-Qādī 'Abd al-Jabbār, *al-Muḥīṭ bi al-taklīf*, 321.

[331] Al-Juwaynī, *Luma' al-adilla*, 102.

[332] Al-Baghdādī, *al-Farq bayn al-firaq*, 329; al-Shahristānī, *Nihāya al-aqdām*, 288.

The argument of *ḥudūth* limited the interpretation of the Qur'anic verse of command. It does not allow for the understanding that God's creative power proceeds from and is a feature of His divine command. An interesting example from the classical theological literature illustrates the consequence of this loss. Arguments for the eternality of divine speech sometimes take this form: "If the Qur'an was created, God should have commanded it to 'Be!' However, this is not the case, for the Qur'an itself is a word containing the divine commands."[333] Here the traditional theology, in advocating the eternality of divine speech, overlooks the fact that the command "Be!" is a speech act like any other verse in the Qur'an. It is no different from the uttering of any specific verses; both are speech acts that occur within temporality and not in an eternal beyond. Furthermore, the literature of classical theology attempting to prove the divine attribute of speech asserts that "God definitely speaks, since religious commandments are His imperative speech."[334] But here the divine speech is limited to God's religious commands, and it does not even occur to the classical theologians that His creative commands might be similar.

The characteristics of God's creative speech have remained far from thought, so far that the Ash'arī theologians even avoided the word *takwīn* (the divine act of creation) in their attempt to eliminate any sense of temporality that the word "act" implies. Instead, they defined the divine act of creation as the "relevance" of divine power to created things, hoping that this speculative definition would help to maneuver around the theological problem of time.[335] On the other hand, Māturīdī theologians applied the argument of *ḥudūth* to the act of creation. They did not avoid the word *takwīn,* for the problem cannot be avoided simply by ignoring a single word, but maintained its standard definition, stating that *takwīn* is eternally a single attribute.[336] This definition unintelligibly equates an attribute with an act. Disturbed by the inconvenience of trying to define the divine act of creation as eternal, Abū Manṣūr al-Māturīdī ultimately argues that

---

[333] Al-Ash'arī, *al-Luma'*, 33; al-Bayhaqī, *al-I'tiqād*, 75.
[334] Al-Ghaznawī, *Uṣūl al-dīn*, 101.
[335] Al-Ghazzālī, *al-Iqtiṣād*, 81; al-Rāzī, *Ma'ālim uṣūl al-dīn*, 47.
[336] Al-Nasafī, *al-Tamhīd*, 28; 'Alī al-Qārī, *Sharḥ Kitāb al-Fiqh al-akbar*, I, 36.

God's act of creation is a mystery. To him, the way of the divine creation cannot be questioned since God carries out His will through His Person (*bi dhātihi*).[337] But al-Māturīdī overlooks the fact that the Qur'an explains all mysteries of creation, clearly teaching that God carries out His will through His command, not through His Person. What might have compelled the great theologian towards this speculation? Surely it is the argument of *ḥudūth*—the false obstacle that makes it impossible to clearly articulate any of the divine attributes pertaining to creation.

2. The Transcendent Quality of the Divine Speech

With respect to its creative power, the divine speech cannot be compared to any kind of speech we are familiar with. We know of no other speech whose direct outcome is actual creation. Therefore, the coming into existence of nature by the divine command demonstrates the transcendent quality of the divine speech. Not that it exists outside of time, but that it exists in time in a way unlike any other speech. God's speech encompasses the universal space and its power summons nature into reality. It is this transcendence that makes God's creative command imperceptible to us. Although creation occurs before our eyes, its ultimate cause remains unseen. In this regard, the mode of divine speech is called *waḥy* in the Qur'an, denoting the way of the divine revelation.[338] *Waḥy* literally means an instantaneous, intimate communication, such as an "inspiration."[339] A picture of the transcendent character of the creative command can be found in the Qur'an's account of the creation of the honey bee:

> *And your Lord inspired the bee: Build yourself houses in the mountains and trees and what people construct; then feed on all kinds of fruit and follow the ways made easy for you by your Lord.*[340]

[337] Al-Māturīdī, *al-Tawḥīd*, 76, 127.
[338] Qur'an 4:163; 11:37; 41:12; 42:51, 52; 53:4; 72:1; 99:5.
[339] Rāghib al-Isfahānī, *al-Mufradāt*, "wḥy" entry.
[340] Qur'an 16:68-69.

The behaviors commanded (building hives and collecting nectar) here describe the innate nature of the honey bee in actuality. Allegorically, this verse explains the natural processes of the honey bee as the result of God's creative command. The creation of the honey bee and its anatomical and physiological traits (that is, the development of the larvae) is ultimately the result of a divine command. Here the Qur'an presents by way of example a general truth: the creative cause undergirding all natural occurrences is the divinely commanded word.

The divine command ensures a particular creation for everything. It specifically determines, regulates, and constitutes the existence of a variety of natural processes. This suggests that a special and elaborate knowledge gives structure to the creative command. All of the functional structures in nature are specifically provided for by the elaborate Wisdom structuring the divine command itself. To return to the example above, the divinely commanded existence of the honey bee demonstrates the perfect wisdom of God, in which the complete design of the species had already been elaborated. Likewise, the verse of command is to be read in this allegorical way. That is, the divine imperative "Be," is not a single syllable uttered without content. Instead, it is a metaphor for the divine command that enunciates all of the specific content of creation according to the perfect knowledge of the Creator. In short, the word "Be" merely signifies the ease of God's creation. He needs only to express His imperative intent and creation is accomplished. God does not create all of the intricacies of nature with the utterance of a single word. Instead, God commands each particular creature, process, and natural relationship to exist with absolute authority as if this required no more exertion than the utterance of a simple syllable: "Be."

Thus the divine command reveals both power and knowledge. It is the ultimate source of all natural force, and of the order inherent in nature that we come to discover. Various examples of the creative command of God mentioned in the Qur'an clarify this interpretation. When the Prophet Abraham (peace be upon him) was about to be put in fire by the idolaters, the following divine command was revealed:

"Fire, be cool and safe for Abraham."[341] This order must be understood allegorically. In reality, a booming voice did not speak to the fire. This verb corresponds to the "be" in the verse of command. God's creative command was expressed in the extraordinary behavior of the fire. Or to take another example: an extremely sinful community was turned into a group of animals when God commanded, *"Be apes, despised and rejected."*[342] Here the verb "be" again corresponds to the verb in the verse of command, allegorically expressing the fulfillment of God's will. Whether the transformation was of the nature of their body or of their soul, this transformation reveals the creative power of the divine command. Needless to say, God did not address to the people in order to demand such transformation. In a third example, the extraordinary creation of Jesus is compared to the creation of Adam, peace be upon both of them:

> *In God's eyes, Jesus is like Adam: He created him from dust, then said to him, "Be," and he was.*[343]

The verse teaches that even exceptional creations are results of the divine command. A transcendent imperative brought both men into existence. Although the two different acts of creation involved two different historical processes, both occurred according to the same ultimate cause: the willed speech of God.

In the Qur'an, the divine command is repeatedly compared to the irresistible order of a powerful authority. If the allegory here is not recognized, then it could be falsely concluded that God demands that His intention be brought about by various autonomous agents of nature rather than by the sheer force of His command. This is clearly a misconception. God's creative command does not demand conformity from an already existing, independent substance, but rather it brings this substance into existence. For instance, a story in the Qur'an tells of a group of people in the past who fled their country—escaping a plague, according to an account in commentaries—but were destined

[341] Qur'an 21:69.
[342] Qur'an 2:65; 7:166.
[343] Qur'an 3:59.

for death. God said to these people, "Die!" and they did.[344] This command is of course not interpreted as a demand for their suicide. It is rather the command that instantaneously determines their death. The style of the narrative is again allegorical.[345] In another example, God commanded the mountains and the birds to attend Prophet David's celebration of the praise of God:

> *You mountains, echo God's praises together with him, and you birds, too.*[346]

The mountains and the birds are not conscious creatures that could understand the divine address; the representation is an allegory. In actuality, it signifies God's creative authority over the unique situation of the mountains and the birds concerning the celebration and praise of God. The divine command caused the mountains and the birds to act immediately as God willed.[347] God's command that ended the flood of Noah and turned nature back to its normal course is also described metaphorically:

> *Then it was said, "Earth, swallow up your water, and sky, hold back." The water subsided and the command was fulfilled. The Ark settled on Mount Judi, and it was said, "Away with those evildoing people!"*[348]

The statement does not mean that God spoke to the earth and sky. It rather means that by His speech, God created conditions in the sky and the earth for the ceasing of the flood. Similarly, the curse against wrongdoers is an allegorical expression of the divine command that fulfilled their devastation. It is surely not a sentence that echoed in the sky.[349] God's bestowal of a beautiful country upon the historical people of Sheba offers yet another example:

---

[344] Qur'an 2:243.
[345] See Abū al-Su'ūd, *Irshād al-'aql al-salīm*, I, 237.
[346] Qur'an 34:10.
[347] See Abū al-Su'ūd, ibid., VII, 124.
[348] Qur'an 11:44.
[349] See al-Ālūsī, *Rūḥ al-ma'ānī*, XII, 94-95.

> *There was a sign for the people of Sheba in their homeland: two gardens to right and left: Eat from the bounty of your Lord and give Him thanks—a goodly town and a Lord all-forgiving.*[350]

The command is in actuality not a vocal admonition. Instead, the order to "eat" signifies the manifestation of divine bounty created in the pleasant country. Likewise, the order to "give thanks" signifies the moral requirement that inheres in all such divine provision. The story of the ungrateful people of Sheba continues:

> *Between them and the towns We had blessed, We placed towns in a row, and We made them easy of access: "Travel therein by night and day, in safety." But they said, "Our Lord, make the distance between our journey posts so longer!"*[351]

In the statement, the order to "travel" signifies that natural conditions were created to allow for a secure trip. It is an allegorical expression of the creative command that generated such conditions. In the same way, the people's request to the Lord is obviously not a verbal condemnation against themselves. It is rather a metaphorical expression of way in which ingratitude caused the deterioration of the travel conditions.[352] In a final example, the constitution of the heaven and the earth by God's command is told in the Qur'an as follows:

> *Then He turned to the sky, which was smoke, and said to it and the earth, "Come, willing or unwilling!" They said, "We have come willingly."*[353]

This depiction of the sky and the earth as conscious individuals does not relate a conversation that occurred between God and the cosmos. Instead, it signifies that God's imperative speech is the authority that organized the heavens and the earth in the beginning. Of course the response of the heavens and the earth in this verse is not a verbal reply, either. It is again a metaphor for the irresistible effect of the

---

[350] Qur'an 34:15.
[351] Qur'an 34:18-19.
[352] See al-Rāzī, *al-Tafsīr al-kabīr*, XXV, 219.
[353] Qur'an 41:11.

divine command on creation. What is expressed is the necessity of universe in accordance with God's relevant command.

3. The Universal Influence of the Divine Speech

The creative power of divine speech is the perennial cause of the existence of nature. The Qur'an considers all natural occurrences in all times to be performances of the divine command. For instance, the sentence, "*We sent down iron,*"[354] identifies the existence of the metal as the result of a single work of the Creator. The figurative phrase, "sending down" signifies the sublime command through which God bestowed the metal upon humankind.[355] In the same way, the divine command is exhibited in the past, the present, and the future. God raised the heavens without any pillars.[356] He adorned the heaven with stars.[357] He spread the earth out like a carpet or a cradle for the convenience of man and opened roads for mobility.[358] He set mountains on the earth like poles standing firm and poured rivers between them.[359] He vitalized the earth with water and scattered across it animals of all kinds.[360] God sends the winds as heralds of His mercy; He drives the clouds and causes the rain.[361] He shapes the fetus in the womb as He pleases.[362] God will shake the earth at the end of time, move the mountains, boil the seas, darken the stars, split the sky, make the earth and the heavens anew, uncover the graves, and revive the dead for the final judgment.[363]

Whether past, present, or future, nature always owes its existence to the creative authority of the divine command. The principle of existence is the same at all times. For instance, the formation of

[354] Qur'an 57:25.
[355] See Abū al-Su'ūd, *Irshād al-'aql al-salīm*, VIII, 212.
[356] Qur'an 13:2.
[357] Qur'an 37:6; 41:12.
[358] Qur'an 20:53; 51:48.
[359] Qur'an 13:3; 16:15; 27:61.
[360] Qur'an 2:164; 31:10.
[361] Qur'an 7:57; 30:48; 32:27.
[362] Qur'an 3:6.
[363] Qur'an 14:48; 81:1-14; 82:1-5; 99:1-8.

the planet earth in the beginning and its current rotation around the sun are both equally the results of a divine command. However, the divine command exerts a diverse influence according to the diverse modes of existence. The modes of the divine command ensuring the establishment of the universe are not identical to those that ensure its ongoing operation.

> *Your Lord is God, who created the heavens and earth in six Days, then ascended the throne. He makes the night cover the day in swift pursuit. He created the sun, moon, and stars to be subservient to His command. All creation and command belong to Him. Blessed be God, Lord of the worlds!*[364]

In the Qur'anic statement, the phrase "all creation and command" corresponds to the complimentary phenomena of the construction and operation of the universe. Although the essence of the divine command is the same, its modes and therefore its effects differ according to the diversity of existence.

As God's transcendent speech, the divine command structures the universal space in transcendent manner, and the ultimate reason for natural existence is God's will. This principle of creation offers an answer to the question, "Where does nature originate from?" by referring to the sublime presence of the Creator. Nature originates in the divine command, and the traces of this origin delineate the sublime presence of God. This sublime presence is referred to as His "throne" (*'arsh*), in the Qur'an, and it encompasses the whole universe.[365] The use of the word "throne" here metaphorically references the exalted position of a sovereign from which he executes his will. The comparison suggests that God rules over the entire universe in absolute sublimity.

> *He is the One Who created the heavens and earth in six Days and then ascended the throne. He knows what enters the earth and what comes out of it, what descends from the sky and what ascends to it. He is with you wherever you are. He sees all that you do.*[366]

---

[364] Qur'an 7:54.

[365] Qur'an 2:255; 23:86, 116; 27:26; 43:82.

[366] Qur'an 57:4.

"Accession to the throne" indicates God's sovereignty over the universe.[367] Similarly, the Qur'anic sentence, "*He is the Lord of the mighty throne,*"[368] can be translated as: "*To God belongs the sovereignty of the heavens and the earth.*"[369] These verses teach that God encompasses everything in the universe as absolute sovereign.

> *Truly He encompasses everything.*[370]

The divine command's resonance in the universal space is described in the Qur'an as the "descending of the command from the heaven." The divine word descends from the sublime presence of God down to the earth.[371] Likewise, the divine command extends throughout the universe.[372] Nothing is exempted from this universal command:

> *God is He who created seven heavens and a similar number of earths. The command descends throughout them, that you may know that God has power over all things and that God encompasses everything in His knowledge.*[373]

God's rule encompasses all human individuals and their works. God is with them wherever they are and whatever they do. God is closer to a man than his jugular vein, and He is closer to the man lying on his deathbed than the relatives around him. He is "close" by way of His knowledge, power, mercy, help, and, in short, sovereignty.[374] Consequently, both distance and closeness (or, transcendence and immanence) can be affirmed at the same time. In His Person, God is absolutely sublime and unapproachable, but by His sovereignty, He is absolutely close and immanent.[375]

---

[367] Cf. al-Ālūsī, *Rūḥ al- ma'ānī*, VIII, 199.

[368] Qur'an 9:129; 27:26.

[369] Qur'an 2:107; 9:116; 25:2; 57:5.

[370] Qur'an 41:54.

[371] See Qur'an 2:176; 4:140; 6:91; 15:9; 16:101; 17:105; 39:23.

[372] See Qur'an 32:5; 67:16, 17.

[373] Qur'an 65:12.

[374] See Qur'an 2:186, 214; 3:120; 4:108; 7:56; 9:40; 11:61, 92; 17:60; 50:16; 56:85; 57:4; 58:7.

[375] Cf. al-Māturīdī, *al-Tawḥīd*, 71; al-Zajjājī, *Ishtiqāq asmā' Allāh*, 147.

To relate the whole existence of nature to a supernatural source is to oppose the naturalistic philosophy. For absolute naturalism, the ultimate source of nature is the natural essence, which exists throughout the universe. Therefore, in absolute naturalism, which allows for no sense of sublimity or transcendence, nature collapses into locality. By contrast, the principle of creation absolutizes sublimity by relating the natural existence to the beyond of the universal space. It accepts an absolute difference of position between the Creator and the creature. As nature is the totality of the works of God, He is distinct from nature in His essence and identity.[376] In this respect, all metaphysical discourses that include nature within the divine existence or regard nature to be itself divine should be considered false. One such discourse, religious monism, defines nature as the totality of manifestations of the existence of God. For monists, nature is considered both divine and sacred. In Neo-Platonism, for instance, nature is a form of God's appearance. As the emanation of the divine existence, nature is not identical with God, but it cannot be thought of as distinct from Him either.[377] On the other hand, in the principle of creation elaborated here, nature is not the manifestation of the divine existence, but the manifestation of divine power as a result of God's command.

The Sufi philosophy in part maintains the Neo-Platonic metaphysics in its discourse on "the unity of existence" (*waḥda al-wujūd*). Here God is thought of as the only being and the only reality. Everything is internal to the divine existence, and nature is but an appearance (*ẓuhūr*) or an image (*ṣūra*) of God. This obviously results in a relativized understanding of the divine sublimity. In Sufi terminology, God's appearance through the image of nature is a "self-descending" (*tanazzul*) from His sublime presence. Through this manifestation (*tajallī*), God is present in all "ranks of existence" (*marātib al-wujūd*), which also become the "degrees" of the divine presence (*al-ḥaḍarāt*). Through God's self-descending for appearance, existence unfolds and expands by degrees. This is called by Sufi philosophers "the pervasion of existence" (*sarayān al-wujūd*) or "the unfolding of existence" (*inbisāṭ*

[376] See al-Qāḍī 'Abd al-Jabbār, *al-Muḥīṭ bi al-taklīf*, 155; al-Bayḍāwī, *Tawāli' al-anwār*, 168.

[377] See Majid Fakhry, *A History of Islamic Philosophy*, 27 et seq.

al-wujūd).[378] What pervades and expands is the divine existence, or God Himself as the only reality. Ibn Ṭufayl, the Andalusian mystical philosopher of the 12th century, argued that creatures are not actually separate from God.[379] Ibn 'Arabī, another philosopher from this region, compared the universe to a reflection in the mirror, as if it was the image of God that was reflected in creation. Ibn 'Arabī considered the created universe to be the image of the divine Person.[380] His follower Ṣadruddīn al-Qunawī asserted that the universe is the outer dimension (*ẓāhir*) of God, whereas God is the inner dimension (*bāṭin*) of the universe.[381] To another disciple of Ibn 'Arabī, 'Abdulkarīm al-Jīlī, the universe is like snow and God like the water which defines its essence.[382]

It is obvious that this discourse on the unity of existence contradicts many of the principles developed in the creationist metaphysics. First, it considers nature to be not a work, but a reflection or a shadow. Ibn 'Arabī argued that, in terms of its essence, the universe cannot be thought of as created.[383] In the same way, al-Jīlī considered the attribute of "creation" (*khalq*) to be figurative (*majāz*) with regard to the universe.[384] Consequently, Sufi philosophers regard the expression, "Nothing exists but God" (*Lā mawjūda ill'allāh*) to be closer to the truth than the more widely accepted "There is no god but God" (*Lā ilāha ill'allāh*).[385] Nevertheless, the former expression, as a summary of the Sufi metaphysics, confines the discourse of the unity of existence to the same nonsense as all other monistic discourses. But the absolute duality of subject and object, "I" and "them," resists this unity. One who thinks and speaks of the world cannot be identical to the world. One who can address God in prayer must be other than God. One who speaks of God as "the only being" articulates nothing; the falsity of his

---

378 See Ibn 'Arabī, *al-Futūḥāt al-Makkiyya*, I, 170, II, 76 and *Fuṣūṣ al-ḥikam*, 181; al-Jīlī, *al-Insān al-kāmil*, 28; cf. Toshihiko Izutsu, *The Concept and Reality of Existence*, 75.

379 Sami S. Hawi, *Islamic Naturalism and Mysticism*, 206.

380 Cağfer Karadaş, *İbn Arabi'nin İtikadi Görüşleri*, 145.

381 Ṣadruddīn al-Qunawī, *Fatiha Suresi Tefsiri* (tr. Ekrem Demirli), 155.

382 Al-Jīlī, *al-Insān al-kāmil*, 28.

383 See Cağfer Karadaş, ibid., 69.

384 Al-Jīlī, ibid., 28.

385 Abū al-'Alā 'Afīfī, *Tasavvuf* (tr. Ekrem Demirli, Abdullah Kartal), 71.

logic is revealed by the simple reply, "Who is it then that speaks of God?" In this respect, the Sufi term *al-fanā* (annihilation of one's existence) is merely a phrase, not a meaningful expression. It does not refer to any reality, only to "one's experience of unity in his non-existence." As a result, it is impossible to assign meaning to the discourse on the unity of existence, much less to prove it.

The principle of creation, based on the clear logic of the Qur'an, precisely teaches that nature emerges and appears in the universal space as the powerful effect of God's transcendent command. Some Muslim metaphysicians consider the divine command to result in a "spirit" (*rūḥ*) that encompasses the universe. As the human spirit mysteriously rules the body, the divine command dominates the universe in a spiritual way.[386] Al-Ghazzālī considers nature to be under the dominion of the universal spirit belonging to the divine command.[387] 'Azīz al-Nasafī, a Sufi philosopher of the 13th century, teaches that the spirit of the divine command is the power that operates nature.[388] It seems that what is meant here by the spiritual quality of the divine command is nothing but the divine power evident in its demonstration.

The Qur'an teaches that angels have roles to play in carrying out the divine command. In short, angels are active in the universe according to God's command, and they represent His will purely.[389] In the Qur'an, angels are introduced as dignified servants who work in absolute consciousness of God's command.[390] They render service in respect and obedience to God's word.[391] The Qur'an classifies angels according to the specific works they render in the universe. Some are the "distributors of command" and some the "operators of command."[392] In the literature of classical theology, it is emphasized that the angels who do service in creation are not the performers of the creative act. They simply represent the divine will; the intention motivating their

---

[386] See Charles-Andre Gilis, *İslam ve Evrensel Ruh* (tr. Alpay Mut), 81-82.

[387] Al-Ghazzālī, *Ma'ārij al-quds*, 169.

[388] 'Azīz al-dīn al-Nasafī, *İnsan-ı Kamil* (tr. Mehmet Kanar), 27.

[389] See Qur'an 16:2; 70:4; 97:4.

[390] Qur'an 16:50; 21:26; 66:6.

[391] Qur'an 21:27.

[392] Qur'an 51:1-4; 77:1-6; 79:1-5.

action ultimately belongs to God.[393] In this regard, it should be noted that angels are effective precisely because they do not have any individual power to create. In other words, angels are not God's helpers. They work in the name of God and by His power, not in His place or on His behalf.[394] The Qur'an, for instance, states that some angels protect people according to God's command.[395] The "angel of death" takes the soul according to God's command, and in this way, it is God that takes the soul.[396] The angel of death is an "envoy" or "messenger" who represents God's will to take the soul.[397] Angels are the "means" of the creative act of God, not the "agents." Indeed, a prophet performs miracles in a similar sense, expressing the divine will directly through action. As a work of God and an effect of the divine command, a miracle occurs in association with the prayer, order, or sign of the prophet, who is thoroughly devoted to God's will. The miracle is God's work, not the prophet's. It occurs as the creative effect of the divine command, spoken in the person of the prophet.[398] The prophet simply functions as a means for the command of creation.

---

[393] Rāghib al-Isfahānī, *Tafṣīl al-nash'atayn*, 105, 106.
[394] Birgivi, *Rawḍāt al-jannāt*, 10.
[395] Qur'an 13:11.
[396] Qur'an 16:32, 70; 32:11; 39:42.
[397] Qur'an 6:61; 7:37.
[398] Al-Juwaynī, *Luma' al-adilla*, 124.

Part Three

REALIZATION OF NATURE BY THE EFFECT OF DIVINE COMMAND

I.

The First Creation of Nature

1. The Concept of First Creation

The "first creation" of nature denotes its inception according to the creative authority of the divine command. In other words, the concept of "first creation" refers to the initial construction and organization of nature. Like the initial establishing of a city, the first creation is described in the Qur'an as an unprecedented act of creation in which God brings the heavens and the earth into being.[399] In this sense, the first creation denotes an activity distinct from God's sustained involvement in the perpetual creation of nature and His promised act of new creation in Hereafter.

> *Say: Travel through the earth and see how He began the creation. Then God will bring into being the life hereafter. God has power over all things.*[400]

Although teaching the original creation of the universe, the Qur'an uses the phrase "first creation" to refer particularly to the original creation of human beings. Resurrection in the Hereafter is called the "new creation" (*khalq jadīd*), whereas the origin of humanity is called the "first creation" (*al-khalq al-awwal*).[401] This first creation implies the establishment of nature, since the original creation of the human being occurred in this context.

[399] Qur'an 6:1; 7:54; 14:32; 15:85.
[400] Qur'an 29:20.
[401] Qur'an 50:15.

When speaking of the first creation, the Qur'an does not offer elaborate information about the inner workings of nature. It makes no mention of the natural processes described by cosmology and geology. In short, the Qur'an does not attempt to outline any sort of "natural history." Instead, it discusses God's creation in metaphysical language, drawing attention to the divine wisdom and power present at the foundation of the world.[402] It is in this way that the Qur'an seeks to illuminate the ultimate source of nature.

> *He created the heavens without any pillars that you can see, and He placed firm mountains on the earth, lest it should shake with you, and He spread all kinds of animals around it. We sent down water from the sky and produced on earth every kind of good plant, in pairs. This is God's creation. Now, show Me what your other gods have created. No, the disbelievers are clearly astray.*[403]

The discussion of the first creation in the Qur'an is metaphysical and not historical. Its intention is not to objectively explain natural processes but to elaborate an ethical foundation of life that can serve as a guide to human action:

> *O people, worship your Lord, who created you and those before you, so that you may be mindful; who made the earth a couch for you, and the sky a canopy; who sent water down from the sky, and with that water produced fruits for your sustenance. Do not, knowing this, set up rivals to God.*[404]

Here, the discourse on the first creation is meant primarily to offer moral instruction: to remind human beings of the divine blessing that requires their response of gratitude and respect to God. According to the Qur'an, the whole of creation is a display of blessings to the human being:

> *He created the heavens and earth for truth. He is far above what they associate with Him. He created man from a drop of fluid, and yet he becomes a manifest foe. And livestock He created. You derive warmth*

[402] Cf. Thomas J. O'Shaughnessy, *Creation and the Teaching of the Qur'an*, 53.
[403] Qur'an 31:10-11.
[404] Qur'an 2:21-22.

> *and other benefits from them. You get food from them; you find beauty in them as you drive them home in the evening and as you lead them forth to pasture in the morning. They carry your loads to lands that you could not reach without great hardship. Your Lord is kind and merciful.*[405]

In this manner, the Qur'an directs attention to the aspects of nature that serve human life and introduces an ultimate explanation for them. The Qur'an does not address the curiosity that wants a biological or historical account of the establishment of nature. When the Qur'an ponders "how the heaven was raised high," "how mountains were fixed firm," and "how the earth was spread out," it does so with the recognition that these aspects of creation demand a response of gratitude to God.[406] The "how" in these contemplations is not seeking any historical or scientifically factual answers. Instead, the Qur'an marvels at natural manifestations of the divine qualities that are beyond the scope of such understanding.

The "first creation" in the Qur'an nevertheless refers to an actual, incredible construction. Nothing is overlooked or neglected in this initial creative act.[407] Nature is the gorgeous art of God, and each aspect of the natural world has been beautifully and perfectly made.[408] In this sense, the Qur'an's discourse on the first creation is not mythical but is concerned with the functioning physical systems of the natural world. The Qur'an states, for instance, that God raised the heavens, regulated the movements of the sun and the moon, and established the balance of the earth that makes it suitable for human life.[409] God put constellations in the sky for the sake of the traveler. He set firm mountains on the earth, lest it should shake with people. He created plants in all colors and sent the winds to fertilize them. He brought down the rain to give water to the people.[410]

---

[405] Qur'an 16:3-7.

[406] Qur'an 88:18-20.

[407] Qur'an 67:3-4.

[408] Qur'an 2:117; 6:101; 27:88; 32:7.

[409] Qur'an 55:5-10.

[410] Qur'an 15:16, 22; 16:13, 15-17.

The construction and organization of nature at the first creation included the ordering of natural properties that would make the world suitable for life.

> *Did We not build seven tight-knit heavens above you, and make a blazing lamp? Did We not send water pouring down from the clouds to bring forth with it grain, plants, and luxuriant gardens?*[411]

The descriptions here (i.e. tight-knit, blazing) refer to the stable qualities of nature that were fixed by the creative authority of the divine command. This regulation is referred to in the Qur'an as God's putting things in service for human existence:

> *God is He who created the heavens and earth, who has sent down water from the sky and with it brought forth produce to nourish you, who has made the ships to serve you, sailing the sea by His command, and made the rivers to serve you; who has made the sun and the moon to serve you, steady on their paths; who has made the night and day to serve you.*[412]

The construction and organization of natural qualities speaks to both the "constitutive" and the "consistent" effects of divine command. It is these foundational effects that cause nature to exist with observable regularity. In this way, the world has been set in order, and nature has been "guided."[413]

2. Creation of the Universe

As a part of the "first creation," the "creation of the universe" is the establishment of the cosmic order. According to cosmological descriptions, the universe contains billions of galaxies, each galaxy with billions of stars and other celestial bodies.[414] The Qur'an frequently refers to the establishment of this cosmic order as the "creation of the heavens and the earth."[415] In the Qur'an, "heaven" or "heavens" denotes the

---

[411] Qur'an 78:12-16.
[412] Qur'an 14:32-33.
[413] Rāghib al-Isfahānī, *Tafṣīl al-nash'atayn*, 106, 124.
[414] See Roger A. Freedman, William J. Kaufmann III, *Universe*, 605 et seq.
[415] Qur'an 2:164; 3:190; 6:1, 73; 7:54.

most immense field of the universe that encloses the earth, the sun, and the stars like a layered roof.[416] The plural "heavens" (*samāwāt*) also suggests the panoramic view of the sky.[417] This stratified structure, from the drifting clouds out to the furthest shining stars, is sometimes called the "seven firmaments" in the Qur'an.

> *Do you not see how God created seven heavens, one above the other, placed the moon as a light in them and the sun as a lamp?*[418]

The Qur'an teaches that the entire construction of the universe was completed in only six days.[419] These "days" pertain of course to God's transcendent and eternal life, so the phrase could be read as "six divine days." A "day" (*yawm*) in Arabic can also be used to allegorically depict a short length of time. Thus the purpose of this descriptive detail is the representation of divine power. The grandeur of God's creative power is underscored by the suggestion that the construction of such a gorgeous natural world took only six days.[420] In similarly metaphorical language, the Qur'an compares the length of one divine day to a thousand years of humanity and boasts that all of the heavens were completed in two days.[421] The Qur'anic account of the establishment of the cosmic order includes these bare details in order to express the effortlessness of God's creative action. God created the heavens and the earth for truth, made the darkness and light, and adorned the sky with stars to indicate direction.[422] God set constellations in the heaven, made the sun a lamp, and assigned stations to the moon.[423]

With such rhetoric, the Qur'an speaks of the creation of the universe metaphysically. It does not try to outline the various physical processes according to which creation came to be. The account of cre-

---

[416] Qur'an 2:22, 29; 3:5; 10:61; 21:32; 40:64.
[417] See Abū al-Su'ūd, *Irshād al-'aql al-salīm*, IV, 118.
[418] Qur'an 71:15-16.
[419] Qur'an 7:54; 10:3; 11:7; 25:59; 32:4.
[420] See Abū al-Su'ūd, ibid., IV, 118, IX, 187.
[421] Qur'an 22:47; 41:9-12.
[422] Qur'an 6:73, 97; 37:6.
[423] Qur'an 10:5; 25:61.

ation in the Qur'an addresses a question beyond the scope of historical analysis: by what power and for what purpose did the cosmic order come into existence?

> *Do the unbelievers not see that the heavens and the earth were joined together and that We ripped them apart?*[424]

This verse refers to the visible fact that the earth and the sky are separated from each other. But it also sketches a very brief picture of the history of creation. In the beginning, the earth and the sky must have comprised one single entity, yet the verse does not describe in detail how they were separated, simply that it was God who separated them. In other words, the verse does not attempt to do cosmology or cosmogony.

Cosmogonies are narratives of the initial creation of the universe. Among them, "creation myths" contain fantastic descriptions of the formation of the earth, the sky, the sun, and so forth. Here is the beginning of a standard cosmogony, taken from a Pacific Northwestern Indian myth:

> A long time ago, before the world was formed, there lived a number of people together. They were the Stars, Moon, Sun, and Earth. The latter was a woman, and her husband was the Sun.[425]

Compared to stories such as these, the Qur'an's description of creation is thoroughly realistic. It inquires after the metaphysical meaning of actual entities rather than imagining humanistic relationships between them. Although Muslim societies have entertained various creation myths like any other society, it would be difficult to find an official Islamic cosmogony in the Qur'an. Cosmology, on the other hand, can be thought of as the attempt to develop a scientific cosmogony: a theory of the history of the cosmic order. Such a theory does not involve the ultimate explanation of the universe, nor does it seek to answer metaphysical questions. But despite these "disqualifications," the scientific cosmogony nevertheless contributes to the metaphysical interpretations of the meaning of the universe.

---

[424] Qur'an 21:30.

[425] Charles H. Long, *Alpha: The Myths of Creation*, 36.

The modern cosmology proposes a theoretical "scenario" to explain the creation of the universe.[426] The universe is thought to have emerged at a moment of beginning and expanded over time, with stars and other cosmic elements forming in obedience to fundamental natural forces.[427] The most popular version of this scenario is the theory of the Big Bang, which suggests that the universe began with a massive explosion. Based on the astronomical observation that the universe is constantly expanding, the theory concludes that this expansion must have originated from a single point about 13 billion years ago.[428] The cosmological scenario on which the Big Bang theory depends still contains many unexplained gaps, and it is not considered thorough enough to provide a complete description of the establishment of the natural order. However, it paints a relatively admissible picture of a creation process that lasted for billions of years. But the Big Bang theory does not provide any proof for or against the principle of creation. The theory merely puts forward a scenario, speaking only the language of possibility. Furthermore, the principle of creation relates not only to the emergence of the universal mass, but also to the sustained existence of the universe at all times. At best, the Big Bang theory provides a scientific picture of the creation of the universal mass out of nothing, but it cannot account for the continued life of the universe.[429]

The Big Bang theory appears to contradict the assumptions of absolute naturalism, which takes the universe to be an eternal, closed system. But naturalists complain that the theory has been coopted by the religious notion of creation out of nothing.[430] Many cosmologists attempt to defend the theory's compatibility with absolute naturalism by enlarging the concept of nature as an eternal, uncreated system to fantastic dimensions that could encompass an event like the Big Bang.[431] For instance, Fred Hoyle suggests that at

[426] Eric Chaisson, *Epic of Evolution*, 298.
[427] Stuart Ross Taylor, *Solar System Evolution*, 24.
[428] Joseph Silk, *The Big Bang*, 8.
[429] Cf. John Polkinghorne, *Science and Theology*, 80.
[430] See Joseph Silk, *A Short History of the Universe*, 2.
[431] See Paul Copan, William Lane Craig, *Creation Out of Nothing*, 249 et seq.

the moment of the Big Bang, matter emerged spontaneously. It was not caused by anything, and therefore it is resistant to any attempt at supernatural explanation.[432] Logically null, this speculation is itself a metaphysical assumption and not a cosmological hypothesis; it is a sophist's argument against the religious notion of a created universe.[433] Another speculation constructs a "cyclical model" of the universe. This model assumes that the universe, eternally self-sustaining and self-enclosed, proceeds through infinite cycles of organization and disintegration, through innumerous Big Bangs and Big Crunches.[434] But not all scientists engage in such naturalistic speculations, and many oppose the assumption of an eternal universe. They find it unscientific to speak imaginatively of the meaning or lack of meaning in regard to the cosmic beginning.[435] As a result, it is fair to say that the Big Bang theory has not impeded the spread of materialistic naturalism. On the contrary, the ancient idea of an eternal nature simply finds new speculations in which to express itself.

3. Creation of the Earth

The earth is the field of creation most familiar to us. Earth is our home, and from this very human point of view, it is the heart of the universe.[436] The "creation of the earth" means specifically the creation of this homeland. It is the organization of the natural world in such a way that life is possible. The Qur'an emphasizes that out of the entire universe, the earth was chosen for human existence and prepared for it according to the divine wisdom. God spread the earth like a carpet, laid it out like a cradle, and covered it with the protective roof of the sky.[437] He made mountains and rivers on the earth and opened roads for men to travel.[438] He sent down water from the

[432] Milton K. Munitz, *Space, Time and Creation*, 158.
[433] Cf. Stanley L. Jaki, *God and the Cosmologists*, 65.
[434] Eric Chaisson, *Epic of Evolution*, 32.
[435] See Eric Chaisson, ibid., 33; Milton K. Munitz, ibid., 152, 153.
[436] See Seyyed Hossein Nasr, *Religion and the Order of Nature*, 133.
[437] Qur'an 2:22; 21:32; 40:64; 50:6, 7; 51:48.
[438] Qur'an 20:53; 13:3.

sky and created plants to eat.[439] Everything on the earth He created for the sake of humanity.[440]

> *And the earth He spread out, bringing forth its water and its pastures; and the mountains He anchored: all for your enjoyment, and for your cattle.*[441]

> *We spread out the earth, and set firm mountains on it, and made everything grow there in due balance. We have provided sustenance in it for you and for all those creatures for whom you do not provide.*[442]

The special organization of the earth for the purpose of human existence is referred to in speculative cosmology as the "anthropic principle." From this perspective, the purpose of the universe's development since its beginning has been the existence of the human being capable of understanding it.[443]

The Qur'an is silent regarding the historical processes that shaped the earth. This is a subject pertaining to natural history not metaphysics. However, geological knowledge can contribute to the interpretation of a properly metaphysical position. In modern geology, the earth is considered to be the same age as the solar system. Over time, a crust rich in chemical elements took form, and an atmosphere convenient to life surrounded it.[444] Dating methods used to determine the age of the earth exhibit relatively plausible results.[445] Accordingly, the earth is considered to be more than four billion years old.[446]

Based on this geological description, we can imagine that the earth was created by a slow process of shaping and organizing that spanned millions years. However, the timetable of particular process-

---

[439] Qur'an 6:99; 14:32; 16:25.

[440] Qur'an 2:29.

[441] Qur'an 79:30-33.

[442] Qur'an 15:19-20.

[443] See John D. Barrow, Frank J. Tipler, *The Anthropic Cosmological Principle*, 218.

[444] See Reed Wicander, James S. Monroe, *Essentials of Geology*, 9; Edward J. Tarbuck, Frederick K. Lutgens, *Earth Science*, 296.

[445] See John J. W. Rogers, *A History of the Earth*, 2 et seq.

[446] Reed Wicander, James S. Monroe, *Historical Geology*, 58.

es, the geologically recorded chronology, has little significance where metaphysics is concerned.[447] It is not ultimately important if an individual knows how many years ago a continent or a chain of mountains was created. The principle of creation teaches that the earth was structured by the power of the divine command, and no subsequent chronology is necessary. It is the creative effect of God's command, resonating throughout the geological ages, that has made the earth into a home for humankind.

4. Creation of Living Species

If we momentarily leave humanity out of the picture, considering its exceptional status in nature, then the "living species" of the earth still include a vast diversity of organisms. In a biological sense, an organism is a particular organization of inorganic matter that exhibits certain distinct and complex behaviors, and life can be defined as this organized behavior of matter.[448] According to modern taxonomy, almost 100 million species have existed at one time or another on the earth, and among these only about a quarter million species of plants, and little over one million species of animals, have been identified.[449] The "creation of living species" thus denotes the emergence of this biodiversity: the coming into being of each species for the first time. In the principle of creation, this emergence of organisms occurs by the creative effect of the divine command, regardless of the natural processes that brought them into existence. Metaphysical origins do not essentially relate to biological origins, and in order to comprehend the ultimate meaning of any created species, it is not necessary to know the historical account of that creation.

The Qur'an attributes the creation of all plants and animals to God's will. It simply says that all species were created and spread throughout the earth by God.[450]

---

[447] Cf. Darrel R. Falk, *Coming to Peace with Science*, 61.

[448] See Erwin Schrödinger, *What is Life: The Physical Aspect of the Living Cell*, 76 et seq.

[449] See Edvard O. Wilson, *The Diversity of Life*, 134.

[450] Qur'an 2:164; 6:99; 15:19; 20:53; 26:7; 42:29; 45:4; 50:7.

> *He created the heavens without any pillars that you can see, and He placed firm mountains on the earth, lest it should shake with you, and He spread all kinds of animals around it. We sent down water from the sky and produced on earth every kind of good plant, in pairs.*[451]

This verse relates the obvious fact that animals are distributed throughout the earth, and that plants typically exhibit two genders and grow only with the help of water. When the Qur'an speaks of the creation of species, it is usually in order to demonstrate the divine grace. For example, the creation of the saddle and milk animals is cause for our gratitude:

> *Do they not see that We created for them, from Our handiwork, cattle which they come to possess? We made them obedient, so that some can be used for riding, some for food, some for other benefits, and some for drink. Will they not give thanks?*[452]

In the same context, the Qur'an praises God for creating all kinds of beautiful plants out of dust, for founding gardens and vineyards, and for making fruits in varying tastes and colors.[453]

The Qur'an says that every living being was (and still is) created out of water, reminding us of the wondrous fact that life depends on such a simple substance.[454] Here "water" can signify rain: the "water sent down from the sky" as it is described in the Qur'an.[455] The fact that water is the basis of all living things is manifest in both the resurgence that follows a rain and in the thirst of living things. Beyond this, the Qur'an does not attempt to explain how all living things were (or are) created out of water. It does not attempt to give a speculative biological description of how organisms first emerged, as this pertains to the history of nature and not to metaphysics. When the Qur'an teaches us to look at "how" living beings were created, it encourages us to con-

---

[451] Qur'an 31:10.

[452] Qur'an 36:71-73.

[453] Qur'an 6:136, 141; 13:3; 15:19; 36:36.

[454] Qur'an 21:30.

[455] See al-Ālūsī, *Rūḥ al-ma'ānī*, XVII, 54.

sider the wisdom manifest in their creation, not to research the history of their development.[456]

The explanation of the creation of species given in the Qur'an addresses the question of "metaphysical origin." This fundamental matter should be approached independently of what is called the problem of origin in modern biology. The question of when and by what biological processes a species emerges should be taken up by scientific research in the field of natural history. But questions of metaphysical origin do not essentially relate to a scientific consideration of the history of nature. Furthermore, descriptions of biological origin can neither verify nor falsify a genuinely metaphysical conviction. The principle of creation explains that the metaphysical origin of all species is the creative authority of the divine command. It is impossible to verify or falsify this explanation with any scientific theories. However, scientific knowledge about the emergence of species can contribute to an appropriately metaphysical consideration.

Fossil findings provide the basic historical data for accounts of the emergence of species. Paleontology organizes these fossils chronologically, concluding that life forms have developed in complexity over time.[457] This sequence proceeds from single-cell organisms to multicellular high organisms and is often represented by a taxonomic diagram of hierarchy, the phylogenetic tree, in which species are classed according to their complexity.[458] This diagram, organized around the formal and functional similarities of organisms, does not necessarily mean that species are "relatives" or that they necessarily emerged from each other. Carl Linnaeus, the founder of modern taxonomy, assumed that all species had independent origins. This position reveals the influence of the traditional Christian doctrine of creation.[459] Charles Darwin, on the other hand, suggested a more continuous, developing creation and argued for the notion of "speciation by progress." He theorized that natural selection governed the mutations of one species into another, and thus there exists a real kinship

---

[456] See Qur'an 88:17.
[457] See Ernst Mayr, *This Is Biology: The Science of the Living World*, 149.
[458] See Helena Curtis, *Biology*, 378.
[459] Heinz Goerke, *Linnaeus* (tr. Denver Lindley), 89.

between them.[460] According to this notion, later called the "theory of evolution," the phylogenetic tree is genealogical as well as taxonomical, and its branches indicate shared relationships to an ancestral organism. According to this model, all species must have originated from some first, single-cell creature.[461]

The theory of evolution suggests a three-fold mechanism of speciation: genetic change (mutation), formal and functional differentiation (variation), and the survival of the fittest (natural selection). In this way, millions of species are to have emerged from one another over the course of long geological ages.[462] But when this speculation is tested against the findings of natural history, controversy and confusion arises. There is therefore no standard theory of evolution, just various interpretations and adaptations of the hypothesis.[463]

The mechanism of variation is a major point of controversy among evolutionists. According to Neo-Darwinism, which argues for the idea of "gradual evolution," this mechanism is the systematic accumulation of small mutations. This position, though prevalent in the field, is still unproven and must answer to the objection that a hypothetical "accumulation of mutations" cannot account for the required degree of variation. Lynn Margulis, well known for her studies on the origin of cells, concisely articulates this objection:

> Neo-Darwinism is misleading. I see no evidence whatsoever that these changes can occur through the accumulation of gradual mutations.[464]

Proponents of "emergence" argue that an accumulation of mutations cannot completely account for speciation, since these mutations depend on a mechanism of variation that is not precisely theorized.[465]

---

[460] See Charles Darwin, *The Origin of Species*, I, 73.

[461] See Neil A. Campbell, *Biology*, 433-435.

[462] Ernst Mayr, *This Is Biology*, 190.

[463] See Stephen Jay Gould, *The Structure of Evolutionary Theory*.

[464] Frank Ryan, *Darwin's Blind Spot: Evolution Beyond Natural Selection*, 85.

[465] See Robert G. B. Reid, *Biological Emergences*, 1-25; Jeffrey H. Schwartz, *Sudden Origins*, 1 et seq.

The concluding remarks of a scientific study of speciation perfectly articulate the limitations of this mode of inquiry:

> Until we know more about the molecular machinery of adaptation—that is, what is and is not possible at the molecular level—our models of speciation must remain little more than speculation based on the subjective interpretation of equivocal data.[466]

Unable to provide an airtight explanation for the biological origin of species, the theory of gradual evolution often becomes an expression of personal belief. For instance, the evolutionary naturalist Richard Dawkins defends this theory with fervent insistence: "It is not impossible at all. That is exactly what I firmly believe."[467] In this case, "evolution" is no longer a scientific concept pertaining to the history of nature; it becomes a doctrine of the naturalistic ideology, usually mobilized against the religious principle of divine creation. This sort of "evolutionary naturalism" (or, in short, "evolutionism") is a thoroughly metaphysical belief, although it maintains the guise of scientific theory.[468] The exaggerated repute of evolutionism in academic circles is apparently associated with this deceptive misuse of scientific language. If evolution is truly the "acid dissolving all traditional concepts," it is not "evolution" as a scientific theory but "evolution" as the modern vessel for naturalistic belief that opposes traditional explanations of divine creation.[469] The former denotes a scientific consideration of the history of nature, and the latter a metaphysical assumption about the reality of the universe. It is only this naturalistic belief that attempts to describe the emergence of species as an unintentional, accidental event. According to evolutionary naturalism, the forces of nature are purposeless and unsubordinated to any creative will.[470]

Although it does not provide a complete explanation of speciation, the theory of evolution has no viable competitor in the field of biology. The so-called "New Creationism," a movement that opposes

---

[466] Guy L. Bush, "What do We Really Know about Speciation?" 128.
[467] Richard Dawkins, *The Blind Watchmaker*, 39.
[468] Cf. Michael Ruse, *The Evolution-Creation Struggle*, 4, 275, 281.
[469] See Daniel C. Dennett, *Darwin's Dangerous Idea*, 61.
[470] See R. Bruce Hull, *Infinite Nature*, 26; Richard Dawkins, ibid., 7.

gradual evolution, does not suggest an alternative scientific theory. The discourse of "Intelligent Design" in this movement argues that species are irreducibly complex and therefore could not possibly emerge from the accumulation of small mutations. It is thought that there can be no gradual transition from relatively simple to highly complex life forms. Since the ordinary forces of nature cannot themselves be the cause of speciation, organisms with complex structures must have been designed intelligently. According to this argument, speciation can only be explained as the result of intervention by an intelligent agent.[471] But the "intelligent agent" here is not a defined natural factor, so the concept of "design" does not signify any particular speciation mechanism within the realm of nature. When a supernatural authority is made responsible for the emergence of complex life structures, questions regarding the histories of species still remain unanswered. From this perspective, the discourse of Intelligent Design has little scientific merit outside of its basic logical critique: that there is no way to theorize the biological origin of species as the result of natural forces.

If the scientific concept of "evolution" refers simply to the theory of the progressive emergence of species, it does not verify or falsify any particular metaphysical convictions, and it does not deliver any verdict on the principle of existence. James McCosh, a Scottish philosopher contemporary to Darwin, theorized that God might have created species through biological processes that appear to us as spontaneous. "Chance" variations could be attributed, in an ultimate sense, to God's determination. The progress postulated by the theory could be the expression of God's creative activity in time.[472] As Ian G. Barbour notices, a "random" natural process can, in an ultimate sense, be divinely determined. All forces of nature can then be defined as agents of God's creative will.[473] According to this creationist interpretation, "creation" is a metaphysical principle indepen-

[471] See Michael J. Behe, *Darwin's Black Box*, 187 et seq.; William A. Dembski, *Intelligent Design*, 105.

[472] See Ian G. Barbour, *Religion and Science: Historical and Contemporary Issues*, 64.

[473] Ian G. Barbour, *When Science Meets Religion*, 165.

dent of natural history that in no way contradicts the scientific concept of "evolution." Consequently, the notorious opposition "creation vs. evolution" is meaningless as long as it compares a purely metaphysical idea with a purely scientific one.[474]

In my own opinion, the explanation proposed by theories of gradual evolution is untenable. I prefer the "punctuated" model of evolution, which is sometimes called "Emergence Theory." This model supposes that speciation arises from radical developments in the ancestral organism. Although it does not identify an alternative mechanism of speciation, this theory appears to be more compatible with paleontological findings and more open to alternative considerations.[475] It is obviously compatible with the principle of progressive and continual creation. The phylogenetic tree can now be interpreted as follows: species have been created in a hierarchical and chronological order, each by means of different radical transformations from an ancestral organism. This rapid emergence of species could be compared to the metamorphosis of a caterpillar into a butterfly. And in this model, the idea of a relative kinship among species is preserved.

"Emergence Theory" is simply one possible explanation of the history of speciation. But as a believer, the details of this history are less important than the principle of creation, which attributes the ultimate meaning of every species' emergence to the creative power of the divine command. Indeed, the Qur'an teaches that "creation" is a metaphysical principle and suggests that the particularities of biological emergence are secondary. The scientific questions of natural history are deemed metaphysically insignificant by the Qur'an. From the Islamic point of view, scientific theories of the creation of living species have no intrinsic religious significance. However species might have emerged, and whatever theories may be formulated to explain natural history, the believer is only required, in each scenario, to remember the traditional praise: "*Mā shā' Allāh*" (God has willed so).

---

[474] See Michael Ruse, *The Evolution-Creation Struggle,* 5; Ernan McMullin, "Evolution and Special Creation," 698.

[475] See Robert G. B. Reid, *Biological Emergences*, 363.

5. Creation of the Human Race

The "creation of the human race" designates the coming into existence of the first human individual on the earth. Again, the metaphysical meaning of the existence of humanity does not essentially relate to the history of its natural development. Whatever that history may be, the ultimate question is the metaphysical explanation of human existence. The Qur'an collapses this undoubtedly complex natural process into the declaration that God willed the creation of humanity on the earth and thus humanity came to be.[476] In the Qur'an, the creation of the entire human race is expressed through the creation of Adam, peace be upon him.[477] Adam represents humanity as the first human creature. He is the first human individual mentioned in the Qur'an, and humans in general are referred to as the "children of Adam."[478] He is called a "successor" on the earth (*khalīfa fī al-arḍ*), and he received universal reverence from all angels.[479] As a *khalīfa,* Adam and humankind with him succeeded all previously created things to perfectly represent God's will on the earth.[480] In the Qur'an this responsibility, which Adam introduced to all humanity after him, is called "the trust" (*al-amāna*), signifying the unique mission and responsibility of humanity in the universe.[481] The best response to this entrustment, described extensively in the Qur'an, is willing "submission" (*islām*) and conscious "servitude" (*ibāda*) to God. These attitudes are compared to a servant's complete trust in the commands and dictates of his perfect lord. In this sense, humans are "servants of God" who have been created for service to God.[482]

Although Adam is representative of humanity as a whole, in terms of gender he only represents half of it. In this regard, the creation of the human individual is not complete until the creation of woman.

[476] See Qur'an 2:30; 15:28; 38:71.

[477] Qur'an 2:31; 3:59; 7:11; 18:50.

[478] Qur'an 7:26, 27, 31, 35, 172; 36:60.

[479] Qur'an 2:30, 34; 7:11; 15:30; 17:21; 18:50; 38:73.

[480] See Abū al-Su'ūd, *Irshād al-'aql al-salīm*, I, 81.

[481] Qur'an 33:72.

[482] Qur'an 2:21; 4:172; 6:18; 7:206; 9:104; 16:36; 17:110; 19:23; 21:25; 36:61; 40:60; 51:56.

Together, man and woman depict the integrity of God's creation, as the narrative of creation in the Qur'an explains.[483]

> *O mankind, be mindful of your Lord, who created you from a single soul, and from it created its mate, and from the pair of them spread countless men and women far and wide.*[484]

The human being as successor of creation is not man or woman individually, but the integrity of both together. When the Qur'an states that the human being has been cast in the best mold, it is the beauty of this mutual relationship between man and woman that is praised.[485]

The Qur'an says that the human being was created out of earth (*arḍ*) and dust (*turāb*).[486] Humanity's material origin was the earth in general, and dust and clay are mentioned particularly.[487] These humble materials were used by God in the creation of the human being, whose physical origin is undoubtedly the material of the natural world. The meaning of this attribution is made manifest in the burial of the human body and its dissolution into the earth. The Qur'an teaches that the human being was created out of the earth, will return into it, and will re-emerge from it:

> *From earth We created you, into it We shall return you, and from it We shall raise you once again.*[488]

> *God made you spring forth from earth like a plant; He will return you into it, and then bring you out again.*[489]

These verses attest that it was not only the first human being who was created in this way. Every human being has been created out of earth and dust, will return into them, and will be raised back to life from them again. The Qur'an relates the creation of human beings to both its immediate physical origins and its remote ones. Humanity is creat-

[483] Qur'an 2:35; 7:19; 20:117.
[484] Qur'an 4:1.
[485] Qur'an 95:4.
[486] Qur'an 18:37; 22:5; 30:20; 35:11; 40:67; 53:32; 71:17.
[487] Qur'an 6:2; 15:26; 23:12; 32:7; 37:11; 38:71; 55:15.
[488] Qur'an 20:55.
[489] Qur'an 71:17-18.

ed from earth and dust, while individual humans are created by the sexual union of father and mother:

> *O mankind, if you doubt the resurrection, We created you from dust, then a drop of fluid, then a clinging form, then a lump of flesh, both shaped and unshaped, in order to manifest (the truth) to you.*[490]

> *He knows you best, ever since He created you from earth, ever since you were embryos in your mothers' wombs.*[491]

According to the Qur'an, the creation of the human being was complete only when he was given "spirit" or "soul" (*rūh*) and thus made exceptional.[492] The full human creation is the existence of body and the soul together. "Soul" should first of all signify the distinctive consciousness that constitutes our personality. In this sense, the soul is not the essence of our biological life, but the essence of our being that transcends biological categories.[493] With respect to biological metabolism, the animal and the human are virtually the same. But human personality cannot be defined by metabolic processes. The reality of the soul as an immaterial essence is logically apparent. But the recognition of this division does not clarify how the soul comes into existence or offer any description of what it is. The spiritual creation of the human race is described in the Qur'an as follows:

> *Your Lord said to the angels, "I will create a man from clay. When I have shaped him and breathed from My spirit into him, bow down before him."*[494]

Here the word "breathed" is ambiguous. It refers to the subtle and mysterious process of the soul's formation in a human being.[495] The same is true of the phrase "from My spirit," which figuratively explains the bestowal of consciousness, conscience, will, love, mercy, etc. on humanity.

---

[490] Qur'an 22:5.

[491] Qur'an 53:32.

[492] Qur'an 15:29; 32:9; 38:72.

[493] Cf. al-Farrā, *al-Mu'tamad fī uṣūl al-dīn*, 94, 95.

[494] Qur'an 38:71-72.

[495] Cf. al-Ālūsī, *Rūḥ al-ma'ānī*, XXIII, 330.

These spiritual attributes transcend the scope of physics and make the human being unique among nature. Despite anatomic and physiological likeness, the human being is radically different in kind from the entire class of animals; it is useless to make comparisons between humans and animals in this way.[496] It is an illusion of the naturalistic discourse that takes the human being to be simply one of many animal species. It is impossible to fully articulate human existence with such anti-human assumptions, for there is no biological basis for consciousness, conscience, will, morality, or even the existence of arts and culture. Although subject to it in many respects, the human being transcends the scope of natural science.[497] The French paleontologist and philosopher Pierre Teilhard de Chardin suggests that, although the human being is a part of nature, his spiritual qualities exceed the boundaries of nature.[498] After Chardin criticizes the classical taxonomy for neglecting the realm of spirituality and degrading human beings to the status of an animal species, he suggests an interesting alternative:

> To express the true position of man in the biosphere, we should need in fact a more "natural" classification than that worked out by present-day taxonomy. In the latter the human group appears logically only as a wretched marginal sub-division (family), whereas functionally it behaves as the unique, terminal, "inflorescence" on the tree of life.[499]

Evolutionary naturalism defines the human being as a highly complex animal organism among a variety of "other animal species." This philosophy attributes no privileges to the human being except an expanded mental capacity, supposedly arising from a particularly complicated brain chemistry.[500] This is effectively the animalization of the human person. The evolutionary naturalist Richard Dawkins

---

[496] See Mario Bunge, *The Mind-Body Problem*, 205.

[497] Cf. William Ritchie Sorley, *The Ethics of Naturalism*, 130, 137.

[498] Pierre Teilhard de Chardin, *Man's Place in Nature* (tr. Rene Hague), 15.

[499] Pierre Teilhard de Chardin, ibid., 80.

[500] See R. Bruce Hull, *Infinite Nature*, 28, 143; Eric T. Olson, *The Human Animal*, 17.

begins his book with this sentence: "We animals are the most complicated things in the known universe."[501] Even if the emergence of humanity was the end of the so-called history of evolution as represented by the phylogenetic tree, this would still imply that the human creature exceeds the limits of the animal. A history of nature is meaningful only if it describes the emergence of humanity on the earth, and this emergence is the acquisition of an immaterial essence, namely a soul. The crucial conclusion is that if the soul is a phenomenon that cannot be identified by natural science, then no scientific theory will sufficiently describes the emergence of humanity on the earth.

Through what historical processes was the first human individual created? Regarding the physical elements involved, how was the raw material of "earth" in all its simplicity developed into a "body" with all its complexity? The Qur'an offers no answer, for this question bears no relation to its metaphysical and moral purposes. In other words, since the Qur'an does not present any natural history, there is no room in its discourse for scientific details describing the creation of Adam from the earth. In the traditional religious imagination, Adam's creation is generally thought to be like the making of a sculpture out of clay.[502] The pleasant place in which Adam and Eve originally lived is commonly imagined as the eternal Paradise. But this is simply because the place is called "garden" (*janna*) in the Qur'an, the same word used to denote the eternal Paradise. In contrast to this common perception, a scholarly interpretation could read the "garden" of our first ancestors as referring to a special place on the earth that figuratively represents the eternal place of happiness in the Hereafter.[503]

It is hard to find in the scientific history of nature a clear picture of the emergence of human beings. At best, the theory of evolution suggests that the first man and woman emerged from an ancestral species according to an as-yet-unidentified process of development

---

[501] Richard Dawkins, *The Blind Watchmaker*, 1.

[502] See Rāghib al-Isfahānī, *Tafṣīl al-nash'atayn*, 72.

[503] Ibn Ḥazm, *al-Uṣūl wa al-furū'*, 42; 'Abd al-Karīm al-Khatīb, *al-Insān fī al-Qur'ān al-karīm*, 22.

and mutation.[504] This suggestion provides a limited but interesting speculative glimpse at our biological history. But the dark corners of this history of speciation are much darker with regard to our own species. And when the spiritual dimension of our existence is taken into account, these dark corners become places of absolute mystery.

[504] See Bernard G. Campbell, *Human Evolution*, 285 et seq.

II.

The Continuous Creation of Nature

1. The Concept of Continuous Creation

The dynamic development of new natural entities can be thought of as the "continuous creation" effected by the same divine command that established the natural world. God's continuous creation is His perennial regeneration of nature: from the formation of flowers and fruits in their season to the growth of infants in their time, from the formation of new weather conditions every day to the developing course of life in each society. In the Qur'an, "creation" means more than just the formation of the universe in the beginning. This concept includes the ongoing regeneration of nature. For example, the "creation of the human being" refers not only to the origin of the human race, but also to the unique birth of every human individual.[505] The Qur'an sometimes refers to God's continued involvement in creation a "reproducing" or "remaking."[506] This unceasing remaking of the natural world preserves a likeness to the first creation:

> *Do they not see how God originates creation and reproduces it? Truly this is easy for God.*[507]

The Qur'an refers to God as the "Creator of everything," the "Lord of the worlds," and the "Lord of everything."[508] Everything in the heavens

---

[505] Qur'an 21:37; 26:78; 39:6; 80:18; 86:5.

[506] Qur'an 10:4, 34; 21:104; 27:64; 30:11, 27; 85:13.

[507] Qur'an 29:19.

[508] Qur'an 1:2; 2:131; 6:102, 164; 7:54; 10:10; 13:16; 39:62; 40:62; 44:7; 78:37.

and on the earth belongs to God. He creates what He pleases, and He adds to creation as He pleases.[509] Humanity can have no master or helper besides Him, for no other creator can give them continuous sustenance from the heaven and the earth.[510]

> *Say: O God, holder of all sovereignty! You give power to whoever You will and remove it from whoever You will; You elevate whoever You will and humble whoever You will. In your hand lies all bounty. You have power over everything. You merge night into day and day into night; You bring the living out of the dead and the dead out of the living. You provide limitlessly for whoever You will.*[511]

In this way, the Qur'an explains the consistently recurring existence of nature. The world's constant regeneration is the exhibition of the divine will. The physical processes through which nature is regenerated are not outlined specifically, only their metaphysical meaning is discussed. For example:

> *To God belongs the sovereignty of the heavens and the earth. He creates whatever He will. He grants female offspring to whoever He will, male to whoever He will, or both male and female, and He makes whoever He will barren. He is all knowing and all powerful.*[512]

Theses verses declare that the entire universe is the divine dominion, for God creates everything as He pleases. No physical description of gender determination in the womb is provided, or of how a woman becomes barren. No matter how physical science describes these natural occurrences, their ultimate meaning always points back to the divine will. A physical description of events does not essentially provide metaphysical understanding, therefore such scientific concepts cannot be thought to define, determine, confirm, or deny metaphysical explanations.

Natural science can help us to understand the functions and processes by which the divine command is effective. To take the previous

---

[509] Qur'an 2:107; 3:189; 5:17, 18, 120; 35:1; 42:49.
[510] Qur'an 2:106-107; 6:13-14; 34:24; 35:3.
[511] Qur'an 3:26-27.
[512] Qur'an 42:49-50.

example, once we understand the embryological processes that determine gender in the womb, we comprehend the creative effect of the divine command in a more elaborate way. This sort of understanding is the task of an analytical metaphysics that aims for the sophisticated articulation of continuous creation. Analytical metaphysics is especially important today, when the prevailing naturalistic discourse has obfuscated the relationship between nature and the divine will. The description of nature as a collection of independent and arbitrary functions has been so influential that it is difficult to imagine a world that is not simply at the mercy of physical forces. In the popularly accepted naturalist picture, the infant in the mother's womb is of course still "created," but the creative agency is attributed to immanent physiological functions. What is overlooked is that the very existence of such functions means that they have been willed into being. At all levels, creation is determined by divine authority.

During the foundation of modern science in 17th century Europe, the prevailing Christian theology taught that continuous creation was the existential principle of nature, for the existence of nature was continually sustained by the divine will. God was thought to have absolute authority over nature. The orderly structure and operation of nature was understood as the result of God's consistent will, and divine providence was supposed to encompass the world entirely.[513] But this religious metaphysic was threatened by the emergence of a new natural philosophy that thought in terms of a "mechanical order." The forces of nature were grouped with the laws of motion and gravity, and nature was portrayed as a fully-functional clock that simply needed to be wound once in the beginning. This imagery raised the first suspicions that the sovereignty of the Creator may not be absolute.

These suspicions can be observed in the texts of Christian natural philosophers at the time. Descartes allowed for divine sovereignty only in the establishment of the natural mechanism: God created the cosmos initially and keeps it from collapse into nothingness, but natural events are determined by the mechanical laws of physics. Robert Boyle confessed that the existence of the universe depends on divine power, but

[513] See Augustine, *The Literal Meaning of Genesis* (tr. John Hammond Taylor, S. J.), I, 172, 173; Anna Case-Winters, *God's Power*, 52, 56.

once the mechanism of nature has been founded it needs no interference. Thus the freedom of divine providence is diminished in the figure of a "law-making" God who is merely a "cosmic legislator." For Newton, the mechanism of nature, although intelligently established, may display certain perturbations requiring divine intervention.[514] In other words, the "clock" was made but the job had not been quite finished. In cases of irregularity, the "clockmaker" intervened to fill the gap. In this model, God can only be present in the order of nature as a *Deux ex machina* (God out of machine) or "God of the gaps."[515]

Two developments in the natural science of the time were necessary before the concept of a "nature without God" could really take hold: a law of conservation that would replace the principle of continuous divine creation and a complete law of motion that would remove any "gaps" from the explanation of nature that called for divine intervention. A theory of the conservation of mass was put forward by chemists such as Lavoisier, and the gaps that Newton had assumed in the solar system were soon disproved by Laplace's astronomy. God was thus demoted to the status of "Retired Architect" in the explanations of physics.[516] But in actuality, these advancements simply reduced the multifaceted world of phenomena to the limited schemas of physics. This reduction was twofold: First, the forces of nature were restricted to those that could be described in mathematical terms. For instance, the manifest reality of the power of will, even human will, was ignored because it is mathematically inexpressible. Second, even though many physical forces remained unidentified, scientists assumed that once discovered, they would comply with the known behavior of the "mechanism" of nature. The incomplete picture of the natural world was thus presented as if it were a thorough explanation.

This reductionist approach is apparent in Laplace's physics. According to this mathematician philosopher, Newton's great genius was that he revealed the "laws of the universe" for the first time. In this ideally deterministic model, if all mechanical values of the uni-

---

[514] See Ian G. Barbour, *Religion and Science: Historical and Contemporary Issues*, 16-23.

[515] See Ian G. Barbour, ibid., 35.

[516] See Ian G. Barbour, ibid., 22, 34.

verse could be known for one moment, then the entire future of the universe could be predicted with certainty.[517] Nonetheless, the law of gravity discovered by Newton was only one of the fundamental physical forces; there were many things left to be discovered. Soon enough, these discoveries came. By the beginning of the 20th century, when particles were hypothesized to be the building blocks of the universe, the charm of the old physics had faded. In the new physics, matter and energy are equivalent, and if anything is conserved it is energy not matter. The new physics depicts nature as more irregular than mechanistic, processes are considered to be less predictable, and indeterminacy has been made into an essential law of nature.[518]

The description of nature offered by physics may change, but the meaning of the principle of creation remains the same: nature and all its processes—whether they be regular or irregular, determinate or indeterminate, predictable or unpredictable—are realized by the creative authority of the divine command. This metaphysical constant insists that the forces of nature depend on the divine command in the same ultimate sense as all other created entities. Once forces of nature are ultimately defined as intentionally determined phenomena, or "willed-effects," then all natural events, even those accounted for by mathematical processes, can be understood to be in compliance with the divine will. Can such an understanding be easily grasped? Ian G. Barbour puts the question as follows:

> Today we must still grapple with the problem faced by the natural philosophers: What are the modes of God's activity in relation to the natural order beyond the establishment of its laws? How can God act in a law-abiding world?[519]

What is the proper way to attribute natural events to the divine will, such as the shifting of the winds, the formation of clouds, the growth of a seed, or the division of cells, even as we describe them in the language of physical forces? If the creative effect of the divine command

---

[517] See Ian G. Barbour, ibid., 34, 35.

[518] See B. G. Sidharth, *The Chaotic Universe.*

[519] Ian G. Barbour, ibid., 31.

is made apparent in physical forces, how should we discern the presence of the divine will in natural events?

Modern theologians have studied this question intensely.[520] A common conclusion is that a relevant metaphysics should be founded on the actual picture of nature that natural science more and more reveals, not on the imaginary depictions preserved by certain traditions.[521] This suggests two basic tenets for an effective metaphysics: First, the enduring Creator of nature cannot be a "God of the gaps," because there are no gaps in the regular course of nature that physical forces cannot explain.[522] Second, the Creator of nature cannot be a God who sacrifices His freedom for the sake of natural laws, because such a God would simply be a founder of nature but not its Creator.[523] The God of scriptural religion is the Lord of the universe in all its fullness, not the simply the Lord of things we don't understand. Only an absolutely creative Divinity can provide nature with its religious meaning. Our worship and our prayers are meaningful only when we trust God's absolute sovereignty over the world.[524] As Hans Schwarz points out, belief in a Deity who is not sovereign over nature ultimately results in the deification of natural laws. Praying in such a world is nothing but a deceptive meditation to calm the nerves.[525] As for the principle of creation, the real world is the world in which prayers are answered.

2. Creation of Natural Forces

The forces defined by physics, such as gravitation, function in the regular course of nature. The "forces of nature," however, are not limited to those studied in physics, for physics can deal only with the mathematizable operation of the universe. There are many active forces in

---

[520] See John Polkinghorne, *Science and Providence*; Ian G. Barbour, *Nature, Human Nature, and God*; Nicholas Saunders, *Divine Action and Modern Science.*

[521] Arthur Peacocke, *Creation and the World of Science*, 46; John Polkinghorne, *Science and Theology*, 84.

[522] Cf. Arthur Peacocke, ibid., 78.

[523] Cf. John Polkinghorne, *Faith, Science and Understanding*, 105.

[524] John Polkinghorne, *Science and Providence*, 72.

[525] Hans Schwarz, *Creation*, 226.

nature which do not interest the study of physics, including the "paranormal" phenomena such as telepathy, telekinesis, psychic sight, and magic.[526] And even before these controversial and exceptional examples, the most manifest natural function surpassing the scope of physics is the function of will. With its characteristic freedom, the will cannot be reduced into any physiological categories, and thus it cannot be defined by physics. Activities that are dependent on the will, including various human behaviors, cannot be described, determined, or predicted by physical laws.[527] Consequently, a complete scientific description or a complete scientific theory of nature in terms of physical forces alone is impossible.

The "creation of natural forces" is accomplished by the creative authority of the divine command that brings into existence all of the functions of the nature's fundamental forces. It is commonly accepted that the regular course of nature depends upon the function of certain fundamental forces. For instance, the buoyancy of water is in essence a function of gravity. The combustion of fire can be described as a chemical reaction and a manifestation of electromagnetic force. From the flashing of lightning to the falling of rain, from the absorption of water by a plant's roots to the metabolic work of its leaves, from the rhythmic beating of the heart to the reflex blinking of the eyelid, all events in the general course of nature can be understood as functions of complex systems of fundamental forces.[528]

The emergence of such regular and fundamental physical forces in the universe proves that there is an ultimate source of power. The existence of energy in space represents a curious intersection of physics and metaphysics. The ultimate cause of the existence of energy in space is beyond the scope of observation and subject only to metaphysical explanation. Regardless of the physical definition of a fundamental force, its ultimate meaning remains independent of that definition. For instance, whether gravity is defined according to Newton's equation or Einstein's, these definitions cannot say anything about the ultimate meaning of gravitational force. An ultimate explanation

---

[526] See Eric Carlton, *The Paranormal*, 9 et seq.

[527] Judea Pearl, *Causality: Models, Reasoning, and Inference*, 108.

[528] See P. C. W. Davies, *The Forces of Nature*, 1 et seq.

should be rooted in a metaphysical description of the ultimate source of power. The principle of creation attributes all power in the universe to God, particularly to His creative command. All physical forces must then come into reality as the effects of the divine command, and the space of the universe is the context in which the divine command resounds. From this perspective, the realm of existence becomes the "interface" through which divine power is made physically manifest. The metaphysical appears through physical.[529]

The Qur'an attributes the operation of nature to the creative authority of the divine command: all activity in the universe belongs to God, particularly to His creating and governing will.[530] The heaven and the earth stand because of His command; everything submits to Him.[531] He holds the heaven and the earth lest they vanish, and it is His will that makes them consistent.[532] These general affirmations of divine sovereignty relate the continuous existence of nature to the divine will, and all physical forces effective in the course of nature are considered to be the effects of the divine command. In this way, nature is placed fully in the realm of divine sovereignty.

> *Do you not see that God drives the clouds, then gathers them together and piles them up until you see rain pour from their midst? He sends hail down from such mountains in the sky, with which He strikes whoever He wills, and averts it from whoever He wills. The flash of its lightning almost snatches sight away.*[533]

This verse describes the realization of atmospheric events as a manifestation of the divine will. In an analytical sense, this means that the physical forces functioning in the atmosphere are not autonomous; they depend on the divine command for their reality. However weather conditions are described by physics, their existence must be "willed" and "ordered" (intentionally determined) in an ultimate sense.

---

[529] See Gerald L. Schroeder, *The Hidden Face of God*, 38.

[530] Qur'an 3:154; 7:54; 10:3, 31; 11:123; 13:2, 31; 30:4; 32:5.

[531] Qur'an 30:25, 26.

[532] Qur'an 22:65; 35:41.

[533] Qur'an 24:43.

The Qur'an offers elaborate examples of nature's compliance with the divine will. Concerning the realization of nights and days, the Qur'an says that God wraps the night around the day and causes each to merge into the other. He makes the night cover the day, and He strips the daylight from the night.[534] He brings the sun from the east and makes the daybreak.[535] The physical "cause" of day and night is the spinning of the earth, but these statements suggest that this spinning is itself a result of the divine command. Accordingly, the Qur'an declares that God could cancel the order of night and day or extend either until the Day of Judgment.[536] In other verses, God sends forth the wind that drives the clouds. He irrigates the land, revives the vegetation, and revitalizes the barren soil.[537] He splits open the seed and the grain and brings out the living from the dead.[538] He holds the birds up in flight as they flap their wings.[539] He causes ships to move smoothly over the sea for the benefit of humankind.[540] Since the entire field of nature from the ground to the air, from the land to the sea, operates according to the same physical forces, the whole of nature can be seen to depend on the same ultimate source of power: the universal authority of God's command.

Since physical forces are the manifest results of the divine command, "nature" is passive in the ultimate sense. The "factors" or agents of performance in the language of physics become the "performed works" in the language of metaphysics. According to the descriptions of plate tectonics, it is fault-lines in the earth's crust that "cause" earthquakes. In the language of metaphysics, fault-lines are just as "created" as earthquakes are. Both originate from the same ultimate cause at the same time and to the same extent. According to the principle of creation, the only metaphysically independent agent is the divine command, and the single absolute performer is the Speaker of that command. Therefore, all natural causes can ultimately be attrib-

---

[534] Qur'an 7:54; 13:3; 31:29-30; 36:37; 39:5.

[535] Qur'an 2:258; 6:96.

[536] Qur'an 28:71-72.

[537] Qur'an 32:27; 35:9.

[538] Qur'an 6:95.

[539] Qur'an 16:79; 67:19.

[540] Qur'an 17:66; 45:12.

uted to a single and universal cause. For this reason, God is called *Musabbib al-asbāb* (One who causes all causes) in classical literature. This quality suggests that only God is absolutely effective in nature, corresponding to the concept of the "Primary Cause" in Christian theology. All natural agents are ultimately "secondary causes" used according to the intention of the divine creativity.[541]

According to this logic, the language of physics is appropriate for the description of natural causes, while the language of metaphysics is used for the description of the divine cause. Both can be articulated together without contradiction. Let us take for example the question, "Why do earthquakes happen?" The language of physics makes reference to the faults in the earth's crust and can be understood by people regardless of their different metaphysical convictions.[542] As for metaphysics, the answer must reference the ultimate cause of all geological forces and fault-lines in the earth's crust. In the principle of creation, all geological forces are realizations of the divine command. Earthquakes happen because they are created by God.

This metaphysical grounding of physical forces negates two concepts popular in traditional theology. One is the concept of the divine "interference" (*mudākhala*). According to the principle of creation, nature is thoroughly realized as the result of the divine command, and it is impossible to describe anything in nature as the result of "interference" on the part of God. In fact, "supernaturalism," the belief that God is only occasionally involved in the course of nature, is a thoroughly naturalistic concept. Belief in the "unity of power" (*waḥda al-qudra*) requires all authority in the universe to belong to the divine command and precludes the thought of occasional interference. The idea of the "co-creation" of natural actions by both divine and human powers, originally called *iqtirān*, is also refuted by the principle of creation. According to *iqtirān*, a natural act, human behavior for example, takes place because of the simultaneous influence of divine power and human power.[543] The principle of creation indicates that such "co-creations" are not

[541] John Polkinghorne, *Science and Theology*, 86.

[542] Cf. Peter Forrest, *God without the Supernatural*, 85.

[543] See Abū 'Adhba, *al-Rawḍa al-bahiyya*, 30; al-Lāmishī, *al-Tamhīd*, 101; al-Ghaznawī, *Uṣūl al-dīn*, 168.

possible because the forces of nature (which include human power) are fully subordinate to the divine power and cannot be thought of as partners with God's effective command. For example, the muscular force is ultimately the chemical energy produced by cells and, like any other form of energy in nature, a created effect of the divine command.

Nature's consistent functions, sometimes called the "laws of nature," demonstrate the consistence of the Creator's constitutive will. The constant physical forces that structure the foundation of nature ensure a consistent creation. For instance, the regularity of the gravitational force testifies to the consistency or constancy of the divine command that brings this force into existence. Thus, even the most law-like physical functions are neither independent nor unchangeable. When we confer upon a natural function the status of "law," this suggests a generalized rule, not an absolute determination. A law of nature is a generalization based on limited observations.[544] To assume that an observable natural function is a necessary principle is to succumb to a simple fallacy of generalization.[545] By taking natural functions to be absolutely immutable, naturalists draw meaninglessly absolute conclusions from their limited observations. They do not realize that an absolute predicate attributed to nature cannot be anything but metaphysical, which makes it necessarily unverifiable by observation. It is impossible to scientifically define an absolute law.[546] In the words of Whitehead, the so-called laws of nature are nothing but the temporary habits of nature.[547]

In classical theology, the consistency of God's will is called "God's habitude" (*'ādatullah*). This terminology suggests that when God uncustomarily wills against His habitude, the conventional course of nature changes. In this case, the "law" is broken, and an exceptional natural process emerges. It is always possible for nature's behavior to subvert our expectations. Speaking in terms of causality, a "consequence" expected to happen under normal circumstances may not occur. To use a traditional example, it is possible that a piece of cotton

[544] Rudolph Carnap, *An Introduction to the Philosophy of Science*, 3, 207.
[545] D. M. Armstrong, *What is a Law of Nature?*, 11, 17.
[546] D. M. Armstrong, ibid., 3, 6.
[547] See Stanley L. Jaki, *God and the Cosmologists*, 20.

exposed to fire will not burn, even though this would go against the habit of nature. It is possible that, according to the will of God, the carbon in the cotton will not react with the oxygen in the air. Instead of the typical reaction, an extraordinary exception may be introduced. The consistent will of God may be temporarily replaced by a will that is contrary but still His. Here is al-Ghazzālī's famous statement:

> The succession of circumstances and consequences are not necessary in nature. The cotton exposed to fire, for example, may not burn. [...] For the doer is God. [...] It is He who burns the cotton willingly. The naturalistic philosophers say that the burning nature of fire is necessary, that it does not burn for any will, and that the cotton exposed to fire necessarily burns. This is what we refuse.[548]

Classical theologians agree that all natural consequences are contingent on the command of God; they are not in themselves necessary.[549] Therefore, these theologians refer to the nature of something as its "custom," insisting that nothing takes place simply because it is "in its nature" to do so. The creation of extraordinary situations is always possible. If God wills it, a stone dropped in the air may move up instead of down.[550] This change in the customary behavior of nature is the possibility of miracles. A miracle occurs when God's will runs counter to His habitude.[551] So a miracle is the replacement of an ordinary natural consequence with an extraordinary one. Al-Ghazzālī concludes his remarks:

> Matter allows everything. Soil turns into plant, and plant into animal, as observed. Miracle is the rapid and sudden occurrence of such things by God's power. So was the turning into a dragon of Moses' stick. Here is nothing obscure.[552]

Historically, the absolute anti-naturalism of Muslim theologians is a response to the Aristotelian naturalistic philosophy. As mentioned

---

548 Al-Ghazzālī, *Tahāfut al-falāsifa*, 225, 226.

549 See al-Bāqillānī, *al-Tamhīd*, 59.

550 See Ibn Fūrak, *Mujarrad maqālāt al-shaykh*, 131, 132, 133; al-Nasafī, *Tabṣira al-adilla*, II, 680, 681.

551 Cf. Ibn Ḥazm, *al-Uṣūl wa al-furū'*, 132; al-Isfarāyinī, *al-Tabṣīr*, 169.

552 Al-Ghazzālī, *Tahāfut al-falāsifa*, 232.

above, Aristotle viewed the substance of nature, and thus of all physical forces, to be independent from the creative will. This view is the basis of the naturalistic preference for "essentialism."[553] In the scientific essentialism of today, physical forces are thought to be the necessary consequences of the essential substance that constitutes natural entities.[554] The essentialist argument concludes that unless the quality of the very substance of nature changes, it is impossible for natural functions to change. Hence the laws of nature can never be broken. Water, for example, is essentially a compound of hydrogen and oxygen, and as long as this essence persist, the wet, liquid, transparent etc. nature of water is necessary.[555] Clearly, contemporary essentialists do not claim that physical forces, along with the laws of nature that describe them, are absolutely unchangeable. But they do relate any possible variability to the change of a natural essence. Once this natural essence is posited as independent of any supernatural authority, scientific essentialism becomes scientific naturalism. On the other hand, if it is accepted that this natural essence is subject to the divine command, then the independence of physical forces and the immutability of the laws of nature can no longer be defended. One most severe problem faced by the naturalistic essentialism is its impossibility of articulating the manifestations of the soul (namely, consciousness, conscience, will, etc.) as the manifestations of the material essence of the body. For this reason, any scientific disciplines that deal with the human being as a whole, such as biology, cannot give much credit to naturalistic essentialism.[556]

The complex and unstable processes of nature are more easily related to the free will of the Creator. It is the freedom of God's creation that makes it possible to pray in such a universe. We do not typically feel the need to pray for the predictable natural events that constitute the general course of nature. For instance, we do not pray for the sunrise and sunset or for the coming of night and day, because we have been accustomed to the regular motion of the earth. However, this is not the

[553] Brian Ellis, *The Philosophy of Nature*, 1, 9, 11.
[554] Brian Ellis, *Scientific Essentialism*, 1, 111, 127.
[555] Brian Ellis, ibid., 6, 217, 219.
[556] Brian Ellis, ibid., 168, 170, 177.

case with regard to complex and unstable natural processes. Since the indeterminacy of such events does not allow for confident predictions, the future of the process is uncertain. We feel the need to pray for such things as rain, the healthy birth of a baby, or the efficient fulfillment of a work, because of the inherent indeterminacy of these processes. To pray is to appeal to the divine will that fills the universe and dominates the whole of nature. In this sense, prayer is power. It seems that the power of prayer has been neglected in modern times due to the influence of scientific naturalism. When physical forces are assumed to be absolutely unwilled and not subject to any creative authority, the complex and unstable natural processes collapse into absolute indeterminacy. When God's creative will over nature is denied, there is no sense in praying, for there is no one to pray to.[557]

In the contemporary view of nature, indeterminacy and unpredictability are two fundamental characteristics of complex natural processes; they are even proposed as the basis of physics. According to quantum mechanics, the indeterminate and unpredictable quality of subatomic functions cannot be resolved.[558] This is also assumed of all chaotic events in nature. Indeterminacy and unpredictability are encountered at all levels of natural process: in analyses of metabolism and population, tectonic motions and atmospheric events, human relations and the dynamics of social life.[559] The more variables contribute to a natural process, the more disorder and indeterminacy increases, and hence an irremovable unpredictability emerges.[560] For instance, due to the extremely complex network of atmospheric causes, weather conditions can only be forecast in the short term and can only be hoped in the long.

As a matter of fact, "surprise" is an essential feature of complex systems.[561] In the naturalistic discourse, the surprise that emerges from natural processes is attributed to "chance." What is chance? For

557 Nancey C. Murphy, "Does Prayer Make a Difference," 242, 243.
558 See Tony Hey, Patrick Walters, *The New Quantum Universe*, 21.
559 See Ian Stewart, *Does God Play Dice?: The Mathematics of Chaos*, 2.
560 See Nicholas Rescher, *Complexity: A Philosophical Overview*, 45.
561 Reuben R. McDaniel, Jr., Dean J. Driebe, "Uncertainty and Surprise: An Introduction," 3.

naturalism, chance is the random or at least unpredictable consequence of undeterminable natural circumstances.[562] According to the principle of creation however, "chance" is either a synonym for "unpredictable" or a vain term that demonstrates only a lack of human understanding, since there is ultimately nothing unwilled or undetermined in nature. The fact that we do not or cannot know a particular consequence does not mean that it has not been willed by God. This is a critical point: the naturalistic dependence on the notion of "chance" proves that the ultimate explanation for any natural event cannot be offered without reference to a divine will, either positively as a creationist or negatively as a naturalist.

If physical forces are created by and therefore subject to the divine will, then nature is an absolutely open system and not a closed one. In fact, even without reference to the divine, the openness of the natural system can be observed in the existence of human will. The will is free and cannot be determined by any physical mechanism. This generates a certain gap in the supposedly closed system of nature. Nature cannot be described in the language of physics alone, for nature includes the human being, and the irreducible freedom of the human being can only be approached through the psychological and metaphysical disciplines.[563] With regard to the openness of the system of nature, the relationship between divine will and natural processes can be compared to the relationship between human will and human behavior. That is, voluntary behavior cannot be completely accounted for by the physiological mechanisms it involves, and hence it remains indeterminate. Likewise, God's free act of creation by means of physical forces introduces indeterminacy and unpredictability into the essence of nature.[564] Just as we are not able to "know" how a person will behave, we do not "know" how nature will behave either. We can only assume, predict, hope, and pray. It could be said that the indeterminacy and unpredictability of nature "hide" the freedom of the Cre-

[562] See David Hume, *An Enquiry Concerning Human Understanding*, 98; Arnold Benz, *The Future of the Universe*, 35.

[563] See Karl R. Popper, *The Open Universe: An Argument for Indeterminism*, 78, 114, 122, 129.

[564] Cf. Arthur Peacocke, *Creation and the World of Science*, 134.

ator's act. The origin of natural consequences in the divine will cannot be detected in the physical substance of nature.[565] This causal relationship remains hidden by experiences of indeterminacy, though it can be inferred by faith.[566]

The metaphysical understanding of physical forces can be summarized as follows: All natural functions are ultimately the effects of the divine command. All natural processes, stable or unstable, determinate or indeterminate, predictable or unpredictable, are subject to the authority of the divine will. The stable processes of nature reveal the constancy of God's command and the regularity of His continuous creation, while the unstable processes hides the fundamental freedom of God's creative will. Since no physical entity in the universe can exist independently of the divine will, nature is a thoroughly open system. There are no "gaps" in nature that God must intervene on occasion to fill. The only "gap" is the entire space of the universe, where the Creator brings fundamental physical entities into reality. The law of conservation, denoting the persistency of physical mass, does not affect this ultimate predicate.

> Every fact depends not only on the principle of conservation, but also, and in the first instance, on a principle of creation. Being, then, at none of its stages, is known in its entirety when the positive sciences have completed their work. Its nature and permanent laws are objects of knowledge; what remains to be known is its creative origin.[567]

Finding nature to be entirely dependent on the divine will, this creationist metaphysic sees "nature" itself as the sign of the divine command, instead of searching within nature for signs that would prove the authority of this command. This principle depends on the teaching of the revealed Book, unlike naturalism which can depend only on its own assumptions.

---

565 Cf. John Polkinghorne, *Science and Theology*, 89; Ian G. Barbour, *Religion and Science*, 101.

566 Cf. John Polkinghorne, *Belief in God in an Age of Science*, 72, 74; Vernon White, *The Fall of a Sparrow*, 96; Taede A. Smedes, *Chaos, Complexity, and God*, 179, 180.

567 Emile Boutroux, *The Contingency of the Laws of Nature* (tr. Fred Rothwell), 160.

Let us close the chapter with a thought experiment regarding the metaphysical meaning of physical forces. I have designed this experiment to illustrate four different metaphysical attitudes. The first is the attitude of deterministic naturalism, which assumes that physical forces are not willed and that all natural processes are determined according to their own unchangeable essences. The second is the attitude of indeterminate naturalism, which supposes that natural processes are not fully determinable and predictable even though physical forces are not willed. The third attitude is that of theistic naturalism, which claims that physical forces are principally independent, but there are gaps in nature which make divine interference convenient. The fourth is the attitude of creationism, which holds that physical forces are always subject to the divine will and that the natural process is never independent. Only this last attitude is compatible with the principle of creation:

> Imagine three parallel rivers that are identical at t moment. Three youths (A, B, C), each hanging from the bridge over each river, place three identical pieces of straw (S1, S2, S3) in their respective rivers at the same point and with the same physical values (the same momentum etc.) at t moment. However, C silently says something while leaving his straw. A minute later, we see that S1 and S2 pass through two different points, whereas S3 passes through the same point of the river that S1 did. Thereupon C smiles: "I prayed that my straw would pass through the same point as A's. My prayer has been accepted." As a deterministic naturalist, Einstein, sitting on the slope and watching the experiment, feels bad: "All straws must have gone through the same course and passed through the same point. If the youths do not deceive us, then something is wrong with nature!" As an indeterministic naturalist, Heisenberg, lying on the lawn, shakes his head: "It is so strange that the two straws have passed through the same point. Nature, how surprising you are!" As a theistic naturalist, Whitehead, sitting on the opposite slope, speculates: "Most likely, God has not interfered S1 and S2 by leaving them to their natural course, but has determined the course of S3 according to C's prayer." Sitting on the lawn and reading the Qur'an, al-Ghazzālī, without raising his head, says: "Each straw has gone through the natural course that God has willed. I congratulate C for his faith."

3. Creation of the Natural Environment

The natural environment is the field of nature that immediately surrounds us and is continuously created and regenerated as we live in it. Human existence is so interwoven with its environment that there is no way to speak of one without the other. Humanity cannot be separated from its environment and vice versa; I exist with my environment and it with me. Therefore, the Qur'an speaks of the creation of humanity and its environment together. It explains that the human existence is subject to the divine existence in the same way that the environment is. In order not to be lost in this environment, the Qur'an recommends turning to the absolute Owner of everything:

> *Say: Who shall protect you against God if He intends you evil or intends you mercy? They shall not find, besides God, any protector or helper.*[568]

> *Lord of the east and west; there is no god but Him; so take Him as your Protector.*[569]

The Qur'an provides an ultimate explanation for the coming into being of the natural environment, often drawing particular attention to the regeneration of the air through the creation of weather conditions.

> *God is He who sends out the winds, which stir up the clouds. He spreads the clouds over the skies as He pleases and makes them break up, and you see the rain falling from them. See how they rejoice when He makes it fall upon whichever of His servants He wishes.*[570]

According to the Qur'an, God sends down rain from the sky in due measure to revive the dead lands.[571] He sends the winds to bear the good news of His coming grace, namely, the rainfall. He drives the clouds to a barren land and causes the rain to fall when people have lost hope for water.[572] It is not people who bring the fresh water down

[568] Qur'an 33:17.
[569] Qur'an 73:9.
[570] Qur'an 30:48.
[571] Qur'an 43:11.
[572] Qur'an 7:57; 35:9; 42:28.

from the cloud.[573] God sends lightning to inspire fear and hope. He makes the clouds heavy with rain and sends thunderbolts to strike whoever He will.[574] If He willed it, He could disrupt the weather and bring one's works to naught. If He willed it, He could strike the crop of the ungrateful with a disaster.[575] If He willed it, He could bring the wind to a standstill and the sailing ships would lie motionless on the sea. He could even cause them to sink on account of what their passengers have done, yet He pardons much.[576]

The living members of the natural environment experience the sustaining presence of God's creative command. The Qur'an teaches that God sends down water from the sky, guides it to springs in the earth, and uses it to bring forth vegetation of all kinds.[577] He causes the trees to spring up and guides them as they grow. Crops emerge out of their sheath according to His knowledge. Vegetation sprouts and yields fruit by His will.[578] God splits open the seed and fruit stone, and He brings out the living from the dead and the dead from the living. He brings forth fruits and makes their tastes different.[579] He brings forth milk from animals and juice from fruits. God brings people sustenance down from the sky and up from the earth in due measure.[580] All living things are subject to His will. The conception and birth of children is guided by His knowledge. He controls the course of the fish in the sea and the birds in the sky.[581]

These statements indicate that both stability and change in the natural environment are determined by God's creative command, and that the life given by the environment is His constant blessing. The environment does not provide sustenance by its own virtue, and this sustenance can be withheld in a number of ways according to God's will. The

573 Qur'an 56:68-70.
574 Qur'an 13:12-13.
575 Qur'an 33:9; 68:18-19.
576 Qur'an 42:32-34.
577 Qur'an 16:11; 39:21; 32:27.
578 Qur'an 7:58; 14:25; 41:47.
579 Qur'an 6:95; 13:4; 56:63-64.
580 Qur'an 2:267; 7:32; 16:66-67; 40:13; 42:27.
581 Qur'an 7:163; 11:56, 57; 41:47; 105:3-4.

Qur'an reminds us of what the appearantialistic unawareness makes us forget and advises to submit to the One who rules over nature:

> *Are those who plan evil so sure that God will not make the earth swallow them up, that punishment will not come on them from some unimagined direction?*[582]

Here "being sure" means forgetting the divine sovereignty and being deceived by the stability of nature.[583] Against this false certainty, the Qur'an announces that God has the power to send punishment from the sky or the earth at any moment.[584] With a single wind, God could derail the deceptive stability of nature and destroy everything.[585]

To live in the environment and forget the divine sovereignty is a typically naturalistic attitude. For a naturalist, the regeneration of the environment depends upon a complex series of unwilled events. It is "chance" that ultimately governs the sustained existence of the environment. This naturalistic view is sometimes called "tychism," from a Greek word meaning chance.[586] But from the perspective of the principle of creation, tychism is meaningless: the natural environment is entirely subject to the divine will, which leaves no room for chance. Thus, instead of relying on the fragile order of nature, one should trust in the Creator who sustains that order for His purposes. Regarding the invasion of a region by grasshoppers or the collision of a meteorite, the emergence of an epidemic disease or the discovery of its remedy, the success of a social movement or its decay, the principle of creation teaches the same thing: all that has happened has been created by God. Therefore, to pray to God is to exert an effort in the environment. The human individual not only participates in the process of nature through the labor of his mind and hand, but also by the prayer of his heart and tongue.

According to the Qur'an, the future of the natural environment has already been determined by God. When the purposes of this stage

---

[582] Qur'an 16:45.

[583] See Qur'an 12:107; 17:68; 67:17.

[584] Qur'an 6:64, 65.

[585] Qur'an 46:24, 25.

[586] S. Morris Eames, *Pragmatic Naturalism*, 6.

of existence are fulfilled, God will end the general order of nature and bring about a magnificent new order. This massive event is called *Qiyāma* in the Qur'an.[587] Literally meaning "rise" or "resurrection," the term denotes in the most general sense the cosmic transformation that will occur at the end of days: the collapse of the natural order, its radical renewal, and the revival of the dead for the final judgment. The Qur'an frequently compares this new creation to the first one, pointing out their similar origins in the divine power:

> *Do they not see that God, who created the heavens and earth, can create the likes of them anew? He has ordained a time for them, of which there is no doubt; but the evildoers refuse everything except disbelief.*[588]

But by not relating nature to the divine will, naturalism is without hope for the future of the natural environment and human existence. The most optimistic speculations regarding the future limit the life of the world to the length of the life of the sun. There is no concept of an eternally beautiful and peaceful Paradise in the metaphysics of naturalism.

4. Creation of the Human Individual

Every human being created in its mother's womb enters into an already existing environment. According to the principle of creation, a human individual does not owe his or her existence to this environment, not even to his or her parents, but rather to God who has entirely prepared this context. Because of this absolute debt, gratitude is the essential human duty. The Qur'an frequently rearticulates the blessings of life and calls upon us as created beings to be grateful.

> *God brought you out of your mothers' wombs knowing nothing, and gave you hearing and sight and hearts so that you might be thankful.*[589]

---

[587] Qur'an 2:113; 3:77; 4:87; 17:58; 23:16; 28:42; 39:67; 45:26; 75:6.

[588] Qur'an 17:99.

[589] Qur'an 16:78.

He creates you in your mothers' wombs, form following form in threefold darkness. Such is God, your Lord. To Him belongs sovereignty. There is no god but Him. How then can you turn away?[590]

O man, what has lured you away from your generous Lord, who created you, shaped you, proportioned you, and framed you in any image He chose?[591]

Does the human individual not see that he did not exist before God created him out of a drop of semen?[592] It is not man that creates a being out of a drop of fluid who can see and hear; it is his Lord.[593] God settles the sperm, which appears as a mundane fluid, in the safety of the womb and determines for it a creation from phase to phase.[594]

We created man from an essence of clay, then We placed him as a drop of fluid in a safe place, then We made that drop into a clinging form, and We made that form into a lump of flesh, and We made that lump into bones, and We clothed those bones with flesh, and later We made him into another form. Glory be to God, who creates best![595]

Those whom God chooses He causes to rest in the womb for an appointed time. Then He brings them out as infants.[596] He shapes the human being in the womb as He pleases.[597] He grants female or male offspring to whomever He will, and He makes barren whomever He chooses. He creates whatever He pleases.[598]

These statements all pertain to the metaphysical meaning of creation. In the demonstrations above, the Qur'an describes the apparent facts of human creation familiar to people, and provides these appearances with an ultimate explanation. Regardless of how the formation of the human body is described in embryological terms, its metaphysical

[590] Qur'an 39:6.
[591] Qur'an 82:6-8.
[592] Qur'an 11:51; 36:22, 77; 80:18, 19.
[593] Qur'an 56:58-59; 70:39; 76:2.
[594] Qur'an 40:68; 71:14; 75:40; 77:20-23; 96:2.
[595] Qur'an 23:12-14.
[596] Qur'an 22:5.
[597] Qur'an 3:6.
[598] Qur'an 42:49-50.

description is constant. The process of creation undergone in the womb is thoroughly subordinate to the divine will, and all relevant biological functions are ultimately effects of the divine command. In the language of scientific observation, the human body develops according to an elegant genetic unfolding. A new genetic code, formed through the unification of germ cells, forms the basis for the infant's growth.[599] This is why two fetuses emerging from the same zygote develop into identical twins with almost the exact same appearance.[600] Aside from this remarkable case, the genetic code of every human individual is distinct. Inherited genes are selected in an unpredictable manner from immeasurable possibilities and by means of various combinatory processes such as meiosis. Therefore, it cannot be precisely known what a new baby will be like.[601] The divine will hides in this indeterminacy, and God's creation of distinct individuals remains hidden.

What cannot be expressed by this genetic unfolding is the spiritual existence of the individual. Humans arrive in the world with a consciousness, conscience, and will. The presence of these spiritual qualities indicates that the creation of the human individual is an event that surpasses genetics.[602] Regardless of the particularities of the relationship between spirit or soul and physiological structures, it is clear that spirit is a special quality of human existence that cannot be defined in purely physiological terms. Classical theology refers to this special property as "a pure substance" that permeates the body.[603] Developmental psychology suggests that the potential for spirituality emerges in the fetus before birth, a fact that the Qur'an understands as follows:

> *He perfected everything He created, and began the creation of man from clay. Then He made his progeny from an extract of underrated fluid. Then He molded him and breathed into him from His spirit. And He gave you hearing, sight, and hearts. How little you are grateful!*[604]

---

[599] See Keith L. Moore, T. V. N. Persaud, *The Developing Human*, 36 et seq.

[600] See Bruce M. Carlson, *Human Embryology and Developmental Biology*, 49.

[601] See Keith L. Moore, T. V. N. Persaud, ibid., 16.

[602] See Geoffrey Madell, *Mind and Materialism*, 2, 3.

[603] See Ibn Ḥazm, *'Ilm al-kalām*, 23, 24; Abdullatif Harputi, *Tanqīḥ al-kalām*, 144.

[604] Qur'an 32:7-9.

This statement clearly indicates that the creation of the human individual is only completed once spirit is given. This means that the spirit is brought into existence at the same time as the fetus. Thus, as al-Ghazzālī points out, the idea that the spirit exists before the body is false.[605] On the other hand, the particular way in which the spirit comes into existence remains undefined in the Qur'an. This event is only described figuratively: as God's "breathing" of the spirit. The Prophet, peace be upon him, notes that angels somehow attend to this divine bestowal of the spirit to the fetus.[606] But the essence of the spirit, as well as the quality of its relation to the body, remains unknown. According to classical theology, this relationship is a "mystery" confined to the divine knowledge.[607]

The human individual experiences God's continuous creation in the processes of physical maturity. This continuous creation comes to an end at death, when the body undergoes a radical destruction. But the Qur'an reiterates that human life is not limited to its worldly existence. A new creation is to occur beyond death. When the finite nature is replaced with an infinite one, every human individual will be recreated to experience eternal life.[608] The Qur'an often speaks of the recreation of the human being as analogous to his first creation. The former resembles the latter with regard to the creative effect of the divine command.

> *O mankind, if you are in doubt about the resurrection, We created you from dust, then a drop of fluid, then a clinging form, then a lump of flesh, both shaped and unshaped, in order to manifest the truth to you. Whomever We choose, We cause to remain in the womb for an appointed time, then We bring you forth as infants and then you grow and reach maturity. Some die young and some are left to live on to such an age that they forget all they once knew. You sometimes see the earth lifeless, yet when We send down water it stirs and swells and produces every kind of joyous growth.*[609]

---

[605] Al-Ghazzālī, *Ma'ārij al-quds*, 109.

[606] Al-Bukhārī, "Bad' al-khalq," 6; Muslim, "Qadar," 1.

[607] Al-Ghazzālī, *Ma'ārij al-quds*, 113; Abdullatif Harputi, *Tanqīḥ al-kalām*, 142.

[608] Qur'an 11:7; 38:38-40; 19:66-68; 30:56; 44:56.

[609] Qur'an 22:5.

In the logic of the Qur'an, it is meaningless to think that divine creation in the Hereafter is impossible, for divine creation has been continually occurring everywhere in the world.[610] The Qur'an rebukes such denial with a simple response: He who created the human being for the first time will recreate him in Hereafter; and He who constructed the body for the first time will reconstruct it again in the new world.[611] The recreation of the human individual is often conceived in the traditional commentary as a reassembling of the body from natural substances after it has been dissolved in death.[612] It seems more plausible to imagine that everyone will be totally recreated, and their identity completely rebuilt, through a distinct, rapid, but still natural process. Everyone will regain the physical integrity that death has disrupted.

5. Creation of the Course of Life

Life flows in society through the interweaving of countless patterns of events. The unpredictable dynamic of social life arises out of the limitless complexity of human behavior. Given the complex interactions of an entire society, each cultural development is a surprising emergence that cannot be foreseen in detail.[613] Such emergences are also subject to God's will, and their coming into being constitutes the creation of the course of life. The metaphysics of social life is addressed abstractly in the Qur'an with the proclamation: *"All is from God."*[614] This absolute statement teaches that everything, even the fluctuations of society, is determined by the divine command.[615]

According to the principle of creation, the course of social life is not the result of human will. Obviously we voluntarily participate in the course of life, but it is not subject to our will or control. In other words, we are involved in the creation of the course of life, but we ourselves do not create anything. The power of our individual will is not

[610] Cf. al-Ash'arī, *al-Luma'*, 21.
[611] Qur'an 7:29; 17:51; 36:79.
[612] See al-Rāzī, *al-Masāil al-khamsūn*, 65.
[613] See P. Lemay et al, "Quality of Life: A Dynamic Perspective," 293; Reuben R. McDaniel, Jr., Dean J. Driebe, "Uncertainty and Surprise: An Introduction," 6.
[614] Qur'an 4:78.
[615] Cf. al-Bayhaqī, *Shu'ab al-īmān*, I, 201; Izmirli, *Yeni Ilm-i Kelam*, 330.

a sufficient explanation for any social event, and thus we cannot consider ourselves to be creators of anything.[616] For instance, parents undoubtedly contribute to the growth of their child, but they do not determine this growth.[617] All things in society, including human behavior, take place according to the sovereignty of God, who is praised in the Qur'an as the "Lord of everything."[618]

In the limitlessly complex system of interactions that is society, the part cannot be taken independently from the whole. So if the part is to be absolutely determined, the whole must be determined as well. To have complete authority over anything, it is certainly necessary to have complete authority over everything. In this respect, God's absolute governance over a particular event proves His dominance over the whole of life. This means that all human behavior is subject to the divine will in the same way as all natural occurrences. Otherwise, one cannot speak of the absolute divine sovereignty over social life, for the very basis of social life is human behavior.

Imagine this ordinary sequence of events occurring in the course of life: A job advertisement catches attention of a young person walking in the park. He applies for the job, and while working there he meets the sister of his colleague. They subsequently get married and have a son with green eyes. In this brief plot, numerous events are interwoven so tightly that if any of them (for example, the wish to go to the park or the decision to apply for the job) change, then the existence of the child becomes something indefinite and contingent. Therefore, to relate the existence of the child to the divine will, it is necessary to relate the entire pattern of events, including all apparently voluntary behaviors, to the governance of the divine will. This reveals that human freedom, according to the principle of creation, is only relative. The so-called "absolute freedom" attributed to humanity is incompatible with the truly absolute freedom of the Creator.

As mentioned above, the Muslim concept of *qadar* indicates that everything in existence is determined by God. According to this con-

[616] Cf. al-Nasafī, *Tabṣira al-adilla*, II, 638; al-Rāzī, *al-Qaḍā wa al-qadar*, 41.

[617] Cf. al-Ash'arī, *al-Ibāna*, 83.

[618] See al-Nasafī, *Tabṣira al-adilla*, I, 594; al-Juwaynī, *al-Irshād*, 187; al-Rāzī, *al-Qaḍā wa al-qadar*, 77; Ibn Ḥazm, *al-Faṣl*, III, 54; Ibn Humām, *al-Musāyara*, 119.

cept, all human behaviors and their consequences are subject to divine determination. Human life unfolds within the realm of divine sovereignty.[619] The human will is encompassed by the divine will, and thus it works under the divine tutelage or control. In classical theology, the human deed is considered to belong only relatively to the human agent and is called a *kasb* (acquisition).[620] In the Qur'an, the divine sovereignty over human choices is illustrated in the verse: "*You cannot will unless God wills.*"[621] Beyond this, the Qur'an does not speak of how the divine will encompasses the human will. The specific quality of this interaction between the divine tutelage and the human will is not expressed in the Qur'an. This matter is not available to human knowledge and referred to in Islamic literature as the "mystery of destiny" (*sirr al-qadar*).[622] Due to this mystery, the influence of the human will on the course of life cannot be defined with certainty, and the limit of a person's freedom regarding an event cannot be clearly determined. Two things, however, remain certain. First, since God wills the absolute goodness demanded by His eternal wisdom, any real evil that takes place in the course of life is the result of the will of created individuals. Second, since the course of life is always realized according to divine sovereignty and is not subject to an individual's will, all of the goodness of life is an expression of divine mercy and generosity. In the words of the Qur'an:

> *Whatever good befalls you is from God; whatever evil befalls you is from your own self.*[623]

Regarding the course of individual life, the Qur'an teaches that God is sovereign over His servants. Everything that transpires in a person's life is overseen by God. In this way, all is from Him. Only what God

[619] See al-Māturīdī, *al-Tawḥīd*, 230, 292; al-Nasafī, *al-Tamhīd*, 72, 73.

[620] See al-Bayhaqī, *Shu'ab al-īmān*, I, 210; al-Māturīdī, *al-Tawḥīd*, 226, 228; al-Ash'arī, *al-Luma'*, 76.

[621] Qur'an 76:30; 81:29.

[622] Al-Maqdisī, *al-Iqtiṣād fī al-i'tiqād*, 151; Ibn Abū al-'Izz, *Sharḥ al-'Aqīda al-Ṭaḥāwiyya*, 320; Ibn Taymiyya, *al-Qaḍā wa al-qadar*, 120; Birgivi, *Rawḍāt al-jannāt*, 20.

[623] Qur'an 4:79.

determines may happen. God is the guardian of the believer and is sufficient to His servant. If one will ask Him, He will respond. He sees and controls the actions of every soul.[624] Goodness is in the hands of God. Unless He wills it, one cannot favor or harm oneself or others. People strive, but success is given by God. Help is from God; He gives His help to whomever He wills.[625] He bestows His mercy upon whomever He pleases. He grants bounties to whomever He pleases. All bounty is in God's hands. All people are poor before God, and He alone is absolutely rich and gracious.[626] God is the One who creates the human person, guides him, nourishes him, heals him in sickness, takes his life and revives him again. He grants long life to whomever He pleases. No one passes away without His leave.[627] God rules over the hearts of people. He comes between a man and his heart.[628] Whoever wishes can take heed of the divine guidance and turn to God; yet no one can do so unless God wills.[629] No one can believe unless God allows it. Had God willed it, all people on earth would have believed in the supreme truth and become a single nation. But God lets whomever He pleases to go astray, and He leads whomever He pleases to the truth.[630]

The metaphysical meaning of social life is expressed again in the metaphysical meaning of nations and civilizations, for history flows in compliance with the divine will. The Qur'an teaches that God will not change the condition of a people unless they change what is in themselves. If He wills harm on a people, no one can ward it off. If He wills it, He could remove an entire people from the earth and put others in their place, just as He has replaced former civilizations with the current ones.[631] God is the One who creates the nations and their handiworks.[632] He has given humankind garments to cover their nakedness and with which to adorn themselves, and He has given them ships and

---

[624] Qur'an 4:78-79; 6:60, 61; 9:51, 129; 13:33; 39:36; 40:60; 64:11.
[625] Qur'an 3:13; 7:188; 8:10; 10:49; 11:88; 12:66-68; 39:44.
[626] Qur'an 2:261, 269; 3:73-74; 12:56; 35:15; 42:19.
[627] Qur'an 3:145; 16:70; 26:78-81.
[628] Qur'an 6:110; 8:24.
[629] Qur'an 74:56; 76:29-30; 81:28-29.
[630] Qur'an 6:111; 10:99, 100; 16:93.
[631] Qur'an 6:133; 13:11.
[632] Qur'an 37:96.

animals with which to travel.[633] It is one of His bounties bestowed upon humanity that we are enabled to travel on land and sea. His are the ships floating on the sea.[634] God bestows upon nations prosperous life.[635] From hunting to writing, all human skills and civil attainments were unknown before they came into being by God's instruction.[636]

> *God has given you a place of rest in your homes and from the skins of animals made you homes that you find light to handle when you travel and when you set up camp; furnishings and comfort for a while from their wool, fur, and hair. And God has given you shade from what He has created, and places of shelter in the mountains; garments to protect you from the heat, and garments to protect you in your wars. In this way He perfects His blessings on you, so that you may submit to Him.*[637]

The fact that life flows under the rule of divine sovereignty demands that we submit to God by trusting in Him, turning to Him, praying to Him, and hoping in Him. Thus, "reliance on God" (*tawakkul*, in Qur'anic terms) is considered among the most important moral principles.[638] In relying upon God, one comprehends the relative nature of human will, considers it foolish to rely on human strength, and thus puts trust in God and turns to Him.[639] A very beautiful expression of this attitude is *istikhāra*: the Prophet's prayer to "seek goodness from God." The prayer essentially asks God for guidance in significant decisions by taking refuge in His will and appealing to His power:

> *Oh God! I seek Your guidance by virtue of Your knowledge, and I seek ability by virtue of Your power, and I ask You of Your great bounty. You have power; I have none. And You know; I know not. You are the Knower of hidden things. Oh God! If in Your knowledge, this matter is good for my religion, my livelihood and my affairs, immediate and in the future, then ordain it for me, make it easy for me, and bless it for*

---

633 Qur'an 7:26; 43:12-13.
634 Qur'an 10:22; 36:41-44; 55:24.
635 Qur'an 11:61.
636 Qur'an 2:282; 5:4; 96:4-5.
637 Qur'an 16:80-81.
638 See Qur'an 3:122; 4:81; 5:11; 8:49; 9:129; 12:67; 42:10; 60:4; 67:29.
639 See al-Qushayrī, *al-Risāla*, 163; Sarrāj, *al-Luma'*, 78.

> *me. And if in Your knowledge, this matter is bad for my religion, my livelihood and my affairs, immediate and in the future, then turn it away from me, and turn me away from it. And ordain for me the good wherever it may be, and make me content with it.*[640]

This consciousness of submission is an essential teaching of the Qur'an and a main theme of the Surah of Joseph. In his childhood, a trustworthy dream was revealed to the Prophet Joseph (peace be upon him) that reflected the good end of his life story.[641] This means that Joseph's entire life, the long years seemingly influenced by numerous human choices, unfolded in compliance with the will of God as it was revealed in the dream. From his betrayal by his brothers to his emancipation by the king, countless voluntary human acts occurred by the authority of God's will. And to borrow the Qur'an's words, the actors of the story did not will unless God willed. In fact, the main teaching of the Surah is summarized in an eloquent expression of the principle of creation:

> *God always prevails in His work, though most people do not know.*[642]

---

640 Al-Bukhārī, "Da'awāt," 48.

641 See Qur'an 12:4-6, 100.

642 Qur'an 12:21.

CONCLUSION

In this book, I have inquired how the observed world of nature comes into existence with the Qur'an as my frame of reference. What I have found is what I call the principle of creation—a principle that corresponds to the notion of *takwīn* in classical Islamic theology. According to this principle, nature and all its processes come into reality by the creative command of God. This statement can be elucidated as follows:

1. Nature is always subject to the divine will. All natural processes are willed and determined by God. The divine will does not denote an arbitrary wish, but rather absolute wisdom. All qualities of the existence of nature ultimately originate in the divine wisdom. The divine command, which causes the natural processes to function, is not just the simple imperative "Be" as it has been traditionally understood. Instead, it is a perfectly elaborated command that provides all of the information needed for the natural processes to come into reality. Likewise, the divine command, as a powerful manifestation of speech, generates effects in the physical world that we experience as creation. All physical forces effective in nature are ultimately effects of this command resonating throughout the universal space.
2. The first creation of nature denotes its original establishment. The articulation of exactly when and through what historical processes nature was founded is not the project of metaphysics or of faith. That is why these particular questions are not addressed in the Qur'an, which explains instead the power and wisdom by which nature was established. In other words, the Qur'an does not offer a natural history of the first creation but an explanation of metaphysical meaning. It speaks neither of the age of the earth, nor of how living species emerged. Thus it

is not meaningful for the Qur'an's teaching to be compared with any theory of the history of nature, and it is not possible for the Qur'an's metaphysical teaching to be verified or falsified by scientific knowledge. This is true for the creation of living species as well as for the creation of the human race. Irrespective of the timeline of this creation, the Qur'an teaches that humankind was given a spirit or soul in order to take up an exceptional place of moral responsibility.

3. The continuous creation of nature refers to its constant regeneration. This includes the creation of physical forces, which are ultimately effects of the divine command. The constancy of natural processes testifies to the constitutive will of God and the unchanging nature of the divine command. The laws of nature sketch the general contours of the divinely imposed course of the natural processes. On the other hand, complex and unstable processes of nature, in which indeterminacy prevails, testify to the freedom of the Creator to determine events irregularly. Humanity can appeal to the divine will through prayer with regard to unpredictable natural events. As conscious and willing creatures, we play a role in this continuous creation. But the limits of that role are vague, for our will is always encompassed by God's. Man is not absolutely free; his is a relative freedom. God rules over life with an absolute freedom instructed by His eternal wisdom, while man must take up the responsibility of his relative freedom.

The principle of creation is the foundation of Islamic metaphysics. It tells a Muslim how the world stands and how to stand in the world. For a believer, the greatest question of life, "Who am I, and what is the meaning of all this?" is answered by the principle of creation. This solution is God's grace to the individual who aspires to save his life by learning his ultimate identity. Accordingly, human salvation lies in the consciousness that existence is bestowed by the Creator. It is bestowed first in the creation that occurs in the mother's womb, and second in the recreation for eternity that will occur after death. The first creation makes worship meaningful and necessary. The second creation, divinely promised, is the basis for hope, goodness, and prayer.

BIBLIOGRAPHY

‘Abd al-Karīm al-Khatīb, *al-Insān fī al-Qur’ān al-karīm*, Cairo: Dār al-fikr al-‘arabī, 1979.

‘Abd al-Karīm Zaydān, *al-Sunan al-ilāhiyya fī al-umam wa al-jamā‘āt wa al-afrād fī sharī‘a al-Islāmiyya*, Beirut, 1993.

‘Abduh, Muḥammad, *Risāla al-tawḥīd*, Egypt, 1960.

Abū ‘Adhba, Ḥasan ibn ‘Abd al-Muḥsin, *al-Rawḍa al-bahiyya*, Hyderabad, 1322.

Abū al-‘Alā ‘Afīfī, *Tasavvuf* (tr. to Turkish: Ekrem Demirli, Abdullah Kartal), Istanbul: Iz, 1999.

Abū Dāwūd, *al-Sunan*, Beirut, 1998.

Abū al-Barakāt al-Baghdādī, *Kitāb al-Mu‘tabar fī al-ḥikma*, Isfahan, 1415.

Abū al-Su‘ūd, *Irshād al-‘aql al-salīm ilā mazāyā al-Qur’ān al-karīm*, Beirut: Dār iḥyā’ al-turāth al-‘arabī, 1994.

Adams, George P., *Man and Metaphysics*, New York: Columbia University Press, 1948.

Adler, Alfred, *Understanding Human Nature* (tr. Walter Beran Wolfe), New York: Greenberg Publishers, 1946.

____ *What Life Could Mean To You: The Psychology of Personal Development* (ed. Colin Brett), Oxford: Oneworld, 1992.

Aḥmad ibn Ḥanbal, *al-Musnad*, Cairo, 1313.

‘Alī al-Qārī, *Sharḥ Kitāb al-Fiqh al-akbar*, Beirut: Dār al-kutub al-‘ilmiyya, 1984.

Ālūsī, al-, *Rūḥ al-ma‘ānī*, Beirut: Dār al-fikr, 1997.

Āmidī, Sayf al-dīn al-, *Abkār al-afkār fī uṣūl al-dīn* (ed. Aḥmad Muḥammad al-Mahdī), Cairo: Dār al-kutub wa al-wathāiq al-qawmiyya, 2002.

____ *Ghāya al-marām fī ‘ilm al-kalām* (ed. Ḥasan Maḥmūd Abd al-Laṭīf), Cairo, 1971.

____ *al-Mubīn fī sharḥ ma‘ānī alfāẓ al-ḥukamā’ wa al-mutakallimīn* (ed. Ḥasan Maḥmūd al-Shāfi‘ī), Cairo, 1983.

Aristotle, *Metaphysics* (tr. Hippocrates G. Apostle), Bloomington: Indiana University Press, 1966.

____ *On the Heavens* (tr. W. K. C. Guthrie), Cambridge, Massachusetts: Harvard University Press, 1953.

______ *Physics* (revised text with introduction and commentary by W. D. Ross), Glasgow and New York: Oxford University Press, 1955.

Armstrong, D. M., *What is a Law of Nature?*, Cambridge: Cambridge University Press, 1983.

Ash'arī, Abū al-Ḥasan al-, *al-Ibāna 'an uṣūl al-diyāna*, Riyadh, 1400.

______ *Kitāb al-Luma' fī al-radd 'alā ahl al-zaygh wa al-bida'*, Cairo, 1975.

______ *Maqālāt al-islāmiyyīn wa'khtilāf al-muṣallīn* (ed. Muḥammad Muḥyiddīn 'Abd al-Ḥamīd), Cairo, 1969.

Augustine, *Confessions* (tr. Henry Chadwick), Oxford and New York: Oxford University Press, 1998.

______ *The Literal Meaning of Genesis* (trc. John Hammond Taylor, S.J.), New York and New Jersey: Newman Press, 1982.

Aune, Bruce, *Metaphysics: The Elements*, Minneapolis: University of Minnesota Press, 1985.

Ayer, Alfred Jules, *Language, Truth and Logic*, New York: Dover, 1952.

Baghdādī, Abd al-Qāhir al-, *al-Farq bayn al-firaq*, Cairo, undated.

______ *Kitāb Uṣūl al-dīn*, Beirut: Dār al-āfāq al-jadīda, 1981.

Bājūrī, Ibrāhīm ibn Muḥammad al-, *Tuḥfa al-murīd 'alā Jawhara al-tawḥīd*, Egypt, 1955.

Bāqillānī, Muḥammad ibn Ṭayyib al-, *I'jāz al-Qur'ān*, Egypt, 1951.

______ *al-Inṣāf fī mā yajib i'tiqāduhu wa lā yajūz al-jahl bih*, Beirut, 1986.

______ *al-Tamhīd fī al-radd 'alā al-mulḥida al-mu'aṭṭila wa al-rāfiḍa wa al-khawārij wa al-mu'tazila*, Cairo: Dār al-fikr al-'arabī, 1947.

Barbour, Ian G., *Nature, Human Nature, and God*, Minneapolis: Fortress Press, 2002.

______ *Religion and Science: Historical and Contemporary Issues*, New York: HarperSanFrancisco, 1997.

______ *When Science Meets Religion*, New York: HarperSanFrancisco, 2000.

Barrow, John D., Frank J. Tipler, *The Anthropic Cosmological Principle*, New York: Oxford University Press, 1994.

Bayāḍīzāda, Aḥmad, *al-Uṣūl al-munīfa li al-imām Abī Ḥanīfa* (ed. Ilyas Çelebi), Istanbul: Marmara Üniversitesi İlahiyat Fakültesi Vakfı, 1996.

Bayḍāwī, 'Abdullah ibn 'Umar al-, *Ṭawāli' al-anwār min maṭāli' al-anẓār* (ed. 'Abbās Sulaymān), Beirut, Dār al-Jīl, 1991.

Bayhaqī, Aḥmad ibn Ḥusayn al-, *al-I'tiqād wa al-hidāya ilā sabīl al-rashād* (ed. al-Sayyid al-Jumaylī), Beirut, 1988.

______ *Dalāil al-nubuwwa wa ma'rifa aḥwāl ṣāḥib al-sharī'a*, Beirut, 1985.

______ *Kitāb al-Asmā' wa al-ṣifāt*, Beirut, 1984.

_____ *Shu'ab al-īmān* (ed. Abū Ḥajar Muḥammad Zaghlūl), Beirut: Dār al-kutub al-'ilmiyya, 1990.

Behe, Michael J., *Darwin's Black Box: The Biochemical Challenge to Evolution*, New York: Free Press, 1996.

Benz, Arnold, *The Future of the Universe: Chance, Chaos, God*, New York: Continuum, 2000.

Birgivī, Muḥammad al-, *Rawḍāt al-jannāt fī uṣūl al-i'tiqād*, Istanbul, 1305.

Bourgeois, Patrick L., *The Religious within Experience and Existence: A Phenomenological Investigation*, Pittsburgh: Duquesne University Press, 1990.

Boutroux, Emile, *The Contingency of the Laws of Nature* (tr. Fred Rothwell), Chicago and London: The Open Court Publishing, 1920.

Bradley, F. H., *Appearance and Reality: A Metaphysical Essay*, Oxford: Oxford University Press, 1946.

Britton, Karl, *Philosophy and the Meaning of Life*, London: Cambridge University Press, 1969.

Bukhārī, Muḥammad ibn Ismā'īl al-, *al-Jāmi' al-ṣaḥīḥ*, Istanbul, 1979.

Bunge, Mario, *The Mind-Body Problem: A Psychobiological Approach*, Oxford: Pergamon Press, 1980.

Bush, Guy L., "What do We Really Know about Speciation?", *Perspectives on Evolution* (ed. Roger Milkman), Sunderland, Massachusetts: Sinauer Associates, 1982.

Campbell, Bernard G., *Human Evolution: An Introduction to Man's Adaptations*, New York: Aldine Publishing Company, 1980.

Campbell, Neil A., *Biology*, Redwood City, California: The Benjamin/Cummings Publishing Company, 1993.

Capra, Fritjof, *The Tao of Physics: An Exploration of the Parallels between Modern Physics and Eastern Mysticism*, Boston: Shambhala, 1991.

Carlson, Bruce M., *Human Embryology and Developmental Biology*, St. Louis, Missouri: Mosby, 1999.

Carlton, Eric, *The Paranormal: Research and the Quest for Meaning*, Burlington: Ashgate, 2000.

Carnap, Rudolph, *An Introduction to the Philosophy of Science* (ed. Martin Gardner), New York: Dover, 1995.

_____ "The Elimination of Metaphysics through Logical Analysis of Language" (tr. Arthur Pap), *Logical Positivism* (ed. A. J. Ayer), Glencoe, Illinois: The Free Press, 1959.

Case-Winters, Anna, *God's Power: Traditional Understandings and Contemporary Challenges*, Louisville: Westminster/John Knox Press, 1990.

Chaisson, Eric, *Epic of Evolution: Seven Ages of the Cosmos*, New York: Columbia University Press, 2006.

Chardin, Pierre Teilhard de, *Man's Place in Nature* (tr. Rene Hague), New York: Harper & Row, Publishers, 1966.

Coleman, Richard J., *Competing Truths: Theology and Science as Sibling Rivals*, Harrisburg, Pennsylvania: Trinity Press International, 2001.

Collingwood, R. G., *An Essay on Metaphysics*, Oxford: Oxford University Press, 1957.

______ *The Idea of Nature*, Glasgow and New York: Oxford University Press, 1957.

Collins, James, *God in Modern Philosophy*, Chicago: Henry Regnery Company, 1959.

Cooper, John W., *Panentheism: The Other God of the Philosophers*, Grand Rapids, MI: Baker Academic, 2006.

Copan, Paul, William Lane Craig, *Creation Out of Nothing: A Biblical, Philosophical, and Scientific Exploration*, Leicester and Grand Rapids: Apollos and Baker Academic, 2004.

Crick, Francis, *The Astonishing Hypothesis: The Scientific Search for the Soul*, New York: Charles Scribner's Sons, 1994.

Cristian, William A., *Meaning and Truth in Religion*, New Jersey: Princeton University Press, 1964.

Cupitt, Don, *Creation out of Nothing*, London and Philadelphia: SCM Press & Trinity Press International, 1990.

Curtis, Helena, *Biology*, New York: Worth Publishers, 1983.

Dārimī, 'Abdullah ibn 'Abd al-Raḥmān al-, *al-Sunan*, Damascus, 1996.

Darwin, Charles, *The Origin of Species by Means of Natural Selection or the Preservation of Favored Races in the Struggle for Life*, New York: D. Appleton and Company, 1889.

Davies, Paul, *The Fifth Miracle: The Search for the Origin of Life*, London and New York: Allen Lane the Penguin Press, 1998.

______ *The Forces of Nature*, New York: Cambridge University Press, 1986.

Dawkins, Richard, *The Blind Watchmaker*, New York: W.W. Norton & Company, 1996.

______ *The God Delusion*, Boston and New York: Houghton Mifflin Company, 2006.

Dembski, William A., *Intelligent Design: The Bridge between Science and Theology*, Illinois: InterVarsity Press, 1999.

Dennes, William Ray, *Some Dilemmas of Naturalism*, New York: Columbia University Press, 1960.

_____ "The Categories of Naturalism", *Naturalism and the Human Spirit* (ed. Yervant H. Krikorian), New York: Columbia University Press, 1945.

Dennett, Daniel C., *Darwin's Dangerous Idea: Evolution and the Meanings of Life*, New York: Touchstone, 1996.

Descartes, *Discourse on the Method* (tr. George Heffernan), Notre Dame: University of Notre Dame Press, 1994.

_____ *Principles of Philosophy* (tr. Valentine Rodger Miller and Reese P. Miller), Dordrecht, The Netherlands: Kluwer Academic Publishers, 1991.

Drees, Willem B., *Creation: From Nothing until Now*, New York: Routledge, 2002.

Durrant, Michael, *The Logical Status of God and the Function of Theological Sentences*, London: The Macmillan Press, 1973.

Eames, S. Morris, *Pragmatic Naturalism: An Introduction*, Illinois: Southern Illinois University Press, 1977.

Einstein, Albert, *Ideas and Opinions* (nşr. Carl Seelig; trc. Sonja Bargmann), New York: The Modern Library, 1994.

Ellis, Brian, *Scientific Essentialism*, New York: Cambridge University Press, 2001.

_____ *The Philosophy of Nature: A Guide to the New Essentialism*, Ithaca: McGill-Queen's University Press, 2002.

Fakhry, Majid, *A History of Islamic Philosophy* (2nd Edition), New York: Columbia University Press, 1983.

Falk, Darrel R., *Coming to Peace with Science: Bridging the Worlds between Faith and Biology*, Illinois: InterVarsity Press, 2004.

Fārābī, Muḥammad ibn Muḥammad al-, *Fuṣūṣ al-ḥikma* (ed. ʻAlī Awjabī), Tehran, 2003.

_____ *Kitāb al-Taʻlīqāt* (in *al-Aʻmāl al-falsafiyya*), Beirut, 1992.

Farrā, Muḥammad ibn Ḥusayn al-, *Kitāb al-Muʻtamad fī uṣūl al-dīn* (ed. Wadī Zaydān Ḥaddād), Beirut: Dār al-mashriq, 1974.

Faruqi, Ismail R., *al-Tawhid: Its Implications for Thought and Life*, Herndon, Virginia: International Institute of Islamic Thought, 2000.

FitzPatrick, William J., *Teleology and the Norms of Nature*, New York: Garland Publishing, 2000.

Forrest, Peter, *God without the Supernatural: A Defense of Scientific Theism*, Ithaca and London: Cornell University Press, 1996.

Franz, Marie-Louise von, *Creation Myths*, Boston and London: Shambhala, 1995.

Frankl, Victor E., *Man's Search for Meaning* (tr. Ilse Lasch), Boston: Beacon Press, 1992.

Freedman, Roger A., William J. Kaufmann III, *Universe*, New York: W. H. Freeman and Company, 2008.

Freund, Philip, *Myths of Creation*, London: W. H. Allen, 1964.

Ghaznawī, Aḥmad ibn Muḥammad al-, *Kitāb Uṣūl al-dīn*, Beirut: Dār al-bashāir al-islāmiyya, 1998.

Ghazzālī, Abū Ḥāmid al-, *Iḥyā' 'ulūm al-dīn*, Cairo, 1967.

______ *al-Iqtiṣād fī al-i'tiqād* (ed. Ibrahim Agah Çubukçu), Ankara, 1962.

______ *al-Maqṣad al-asnā fī sharḥ ma'ānī asmā' Allāh al-ḥusnā* (ed. Faḍluh Shahāda), Dār al-mashriq, 1971.

______ *Ma'ārij al-quds fī madārij ma'rifa al-nafs*, Beirut: Dār al-kutub al-'ilmiyya, 1988.

______ *Mishkāt al-anwār*, Egypt: Maṭba'a al-ṣidq, 1322.

______ *al-Munqidh min al-ḍalāl*, Damascus, 1939.

______ *Tahāfut al-falāsifa* (ed. Sulaymān Dunyā), Egypt: Dār al-ma'ārif, undated.

Gibson, Arthur, *God and the Universe*, London and New York: Routledge, 2000.

Gilis, Charles-Andre, *Islam ve Evrensel Ruh* (tr. to Turkish: Alpay Mut), Istanbul: Insan, 2004.

Gilkey, Langdon, *Nature, Reality, and the Sacred: The Nexus of Science and Religion*, Minneapolis: Fortress Press, 1993.

Godfrey-Smith, Peter, *Theory and Reality: An Introduction to the Philosophy of Science*, Chicago: The University of Chicago Press, 2003.

Goerke, Heinz, *Linnaeus* (tr. Denver Lindley), New York: Charles Scribner's Sons, 1973.

Gould, Stephen Jay, *Rocks of Ages: Science and Religion in the Fullness of Life*, New York: Ballantine, 1999.

______ *The Structure of Evolutionary Theory*, Cambridge, Massachusetts: Harvard University Press, 2002.

Grey, Mary, *Introducing Feminist Images of God*, Sheffield: Sheffield Academic Press, 2001.

Griffin, David Ray, *Religion and Scientific Naturalism: Overcoming the Conflicts*, Albany: State University of New York Press, 2000.

Guenon, Rene, *The Crisis of the Modern World* (tr. Marco Pallis et al), Hillsdale, NY: Sophia Perennis, 2001.

______ *The Multiple States of the Being* (ed. Samuel D. Fohr; tr. Henry D. Fohr), Hillsdale, 2004.

Habgood, John, *The Concept of Nature*, London: Darton, Longman and Todd Ltd., 2002.

Hamilton, Virginia, *In the Beginning: Creation Stories from Around the World*, San Diego: Harcourt Brace Jovanovich Publishers, 1988.

Hampshire, S. N., "Metaphysical Systems", *The Nature of Metaphysics* (ed. D. F. Pears), London: Macmillan & Co Ltd., 1957.

Harputi, Abdullatif, *Tanqīḥ al-kalām fī 'aqāid ahl al-Islām*, Istanbul, 1330.

Harris, Errol E., *The Reality of Time*, Albany: State University of New York Press, 1988.

Harrison, Paul, *The Elements of Pantheism: Understanding the Divinity in Nature and the Universe*, Boston: Element Books, 1999.

Hartshorne, Charles, *Omnipotence and Other Theological Mistakes*, Albany: State University of New York Press, 1984.

Hawi, Sami S., *Islamic Naturalism and Mysticism: A Philosophical Study of Ibn Tufayl's Hayy bin Yaqzan*, Leiden: E. J. Brill, 1974.

Hawking, Stephen W., *A Brief History of Time: From the Big Bang to Black Holes*, Toronto and New York: Bantam Books, 1988.

Hempel, Carl G., "The Empiricist Criterion of Meaning", *Logical Positivism* (ed. A. J. Ayer), Glencoe, Illinois: The Free Press, 1959.

Hey, Tony, Patrick Walters, *The New Quantum Universe*, Cambridge: Cambridge University Press, 2003.

Hick, John, *Faith and Knowledge*, Hampshire and London: Macmillan Press, 1988.

______ *The Existence of God*, New York: The Macmillan Company, 1964.

Hooft, Gerard 't, *In Search of the Ultimate Building Blocks*, Cambridge: Cambridge University Press, 1997.

Hull, R. Bruce, *Infinite Nature*, Chicago and London: The University of Chicago Press, 2006.

Hume, David, *An Enquiry concerning Human Understanding* (ed. Antony Flew), La Salle, Illinois: Open Court, 1992.

______ *Dialogues Concerning Natural Religion* (ed. Martin Bell), London: Penguin Books, 1990.

Ibn Abū al-'Izz, Ṣadr al-dīn, *Sharḥ al-'Aqīda al-Ṭaḥāwiyya*, Beirut, 1993.

Ibn 'Arabī, Muḥyiddīn, *al-Futūḥāt al-Makkiyya* (ed. 'Uthmān Yaḥyā), Cairo, 1975.

______ *Fuṣūṣ al-ḥikam*, Beirut, 1980.

Ibn Fūrak, Muḥammad ibn Ḥasan, *Mujarrad maqālāt al-shaykh Abī al-Ḥasan al-Ash'arī* (ed. Daniel Gimaret), Beirut, 1987.

Ibn Ḥazm, 'Alī ibn Aḥmad, *al-Faṣl fī al-milal wa al-ahwā' wa al-niḥal*, Beirut: Dār al-ma'rifa, 1986.

_____ *'Ilm al-kalām 'alā madhhab ahl al-sunna wa al-jamā'a* (ed. Aḥmad Hijāzī), Cairo: al-Maktaba al-Thaqafī, 1989.

_____ *al-Uṣūl wa al-furū'*, Beirut: Dār al-kutub al-'ilmiyya, 1984.

Ibn Ḥibbān, Muḥammad ibn Aḥmad, *al-Sīra al-nabawiyya wa akhbār al-khulafā'*, Beirut: al-Kutub al-thaqafiyya, 1987.

Ibn Hishām, 'Abd al-Malik, *al-Sīra al-nabawiyya*, Beirut: al-Maktaba al-'aṣriyya, 1992.

Ibn Humām, Kamāl al-dīn, *al-Musāyara fī al-'aqāid al-munjiya fī al-ākhira*, Cairo, 1317.

Ibn Māja, Muḥammad ibn Yazīd, *al-Sunan*, Beirut, 1986.

Ibn Manẓūr, Muḥammad ibn Mukarram, *Lisān al-'Arab*, Beirut: Dār Ṣādir, undated.

Ibn Qayyim al-Jawziyya, *Miftāḥ dār al-sa'āda*, Beirut, undated.

_____ *Shifā' al-'alīl fī masāil al-qaḍā' wa al-qadar wa al-ḥikma wa al-ta'līl*, Beirut, 1997.

Ibn Qudāma, 'Abdullah, *al-I'tiqād* (ed. 'Ādil 'Abd al-Mun'im), Cairo: Maktaba al-Qur'ān, undated.

Ibn Rushd, *Tahāfut al-Tahāfut* (ed. Maurice Bouyges), Beirut, 1930.

Ibn Sīnā, *al-Najāt fī al-manṭiq wa al-ilāhiyyāt*, Beirut, 1992.

_____ *al-Shifā': al-Ilāhiyyāt* (ed. al-Ab Kinwātī, Saīd Zāyad), Intishārāt Nāṣir Khusraw, 1363.

_____ *al-Shifā': al-Samā' al-ṭabī'ī* (ed. Ja 'far Ālyāsīn), Beirut: Dār al-mahahil, 1996.

Ibn Taymiyya, Taqī al-dīn, *Kitāb al-Asmā' wa al-ṣifāt*, Beirut, 1998.

_____ *al-Qaḍā' wa al-qadar*, Beirut: Dār al-kitāb al-'arabī, 1991.

Ījī, 'Abd al-Raḥmān ibn Aḥmad al-, *al-Mawāqif fī 'ilm al-kalām*, Cairo, undated.

Isfarāyinī, Shaḥfūr ibn Ṭāhir al-, *al-Tabṣīr fī al-dīn* (ed. Kamāl Yūsuf), Beirut: 'Ālam al-kutub, 1983.

Izmirli, Ismail Hakki, *Muḥaṣṣal al-kalām wa al-ḥikma*, Istanbul, 1336.

_____ *Yeni Ilm-i Kelam*, Istanbul, 1343.

Izutsu, Toshihiko, *The Concept and Reality of Existence*, Malaysia: Islamic Book Trust, 2007.

Jaki, Stanley L., *God and the Cosmologists*, Washington D.C.: Regnery Gateway, 1989.

Jaspers, Karl, *Philosophy of Existence* (tr. Richard F. Grabau), Philadelphia: University of Pennsylvania Press, 1971.

Jīlī, 'Abd al-Karīm al-, *al-Insān al-kāmil fī ma'rifa al-awākhir wa al-awāil*, Egypt, 1316.

Jung, C. G., *Memories, Dreams, Reflections* (ed. Aniela Jaffé; tr. Richard and Clara Winston), New York: Vintage Books, 1989.

Juwaynī, 'Abd al-Malik ibn Muḥammad al-, *al-'Aqīda al-Niẓāmiyya fī arkān al-Islāmiyya*, Cairo: Maktaba al-Kulliyyāt al-Azhariyya, 1978.

_____ *Kitab al-Irshād ilā qawāṭi' al-adilla fī uṣūl al-i'tiqād* (ed. Muḥammad Yūsuf Mūsā, 'Alī 'Abd al-Mun'im 'Abd al-Ḥamīd), Egypt: Maktaba al-Hānjī, 1950.

_____ *Luma' al-adilla fī qawā'id 'aqāid ahl al-sunna wa al-jamā'a* (ed. Fawqiyya Ḥusayn Maḥmūd), Beirut: 'Ālam al-kutub, 1987.

_____ *al-Shāmil fī uṣūl al-dīn*, Alexandria, Egypt: al-Ma'ārif, 1969.

Kant, Immanuel, *Prolegomena to Any Future Metaphysics* (ed. Lewis W. Beck), New York: The Liberal Arts Press, 1951.

Karadaş, Cağfer, *Ibn Arabi'nin Itikadi Görüşleri*, Istanbul: Beyan, 1997.

Lāmishī, Maḥmūd ibn Zayd al-, *Kitāb al-Tamhīd li qawā'id al-tawḥīd*, Beirut, 1995.

Lamprecht, Sterling P., *The Metaphysics of Naturalism*, New York: Meredith Publishing Company, 1967.

Laqānī, 'Abd al-Salām ibn Ibrāhīm al-, *Itḥāf al-murīd*, Egypt: Maṭba'a al-sa'āda, 1955.

Leclerc, Ivor, *The Nature of Physical Existence*, London: George Allen & Udwin Ltd., 1972.

Lemay, P., J-P. Dauwalder, V. Pomini, M. Bersier, "Quality of Life: A Dynamic Perspective", *Nonlinear Dynamics in Human Behavior* (ed. W. Sulis, A. Combs), Singapore: World Scientific, 1996.

Long, Charles H., *Alpha: The Myths of Creation*, California: Scholars Press, 1963.

Loptson, Peter, *Reality: Fundamental Topics in Metaphysics*, Toronto: University of Toronto Press, 2001.

Lucas, J. R., *Space, Time and Causality: An Essay in Natural Philosophy*, New York: Oxford University Press, 1984.

Lucretius, *On the Nature of the Universe* (tr. Sir Ronald Melville), New York: Oxford University Press, 1997.

Madell, Geoffrey, *Mind and Materialism*, Edinburgh: Edinburgh University Press, 1988.

Mālik, ibn Anas, *al-Muwaṭṭa*, Maghrib, 1992.

Maqdisī, 'Abd al-Ghanī ibn 'Abd al-Wāḥid al-, *al-Iqtiṣād fī al-i'tiqād*, Medina: Maktaba al-'ulūm wa al-ḥikam, 1993.

Marcel, Gabriel, *Problematic Man* (tr. Brian Thompson), New York: Herder & Herder, 1967.

Maritain, Jacques, *A Preface to Metaphysics: Seven Lectures on Being*, London: Sheed & Ward, 1948.

Māturīdī, Abū Manṣūr al-, *Kitāb al-Tawḥīd* (ed. Fatḥullah Khulayf), Beirut, 1986.

Mayr, Ernst, *This Is Biology: The Science of the Living World*, Cambridge, Massachusetts: Harvard University Press, 1997.

McDaniel, Reuben R., Jr., Dean J. Driebe, "Uncertainty and Surprise: An Introduction", *Uncertainty and Surprise in Complex Systems: Questioning on Working with the Unexpected* (ed. Reuben R. McDaniel, Jr., Dean J. Driebe), Heidelberg: Springer, 2005.

McMullin, Ernan, "Evolution and Special Creation", *The Philosophy of Biology* (ed. David L. Hull, Michael Ruse), Oxford and New York: Oxford University Press, 1998.

Mitchell, Basil, *The Justification of Religious Belief*, London: The Macmillan Press, 1973.

Monod, Jacques, *Chance and Necessity: An Essay on the Natural Philosophy of Modern Biology* (tr. Austryn Wainhouse), New York: Alfred A. Knopf, 1971.

Montaigne, *The Essays of Montaigne* (tr. E.J. Trechmann), New York: The Modern Library, 1946.

Moore, Keith L., T. V. N. Persaud, *The Developing Human: Clinically Oriented Emryology*, Philadelphia: Saunders, 2003.

Morris, Richard, *The Fate of the Universe*, New York: Playboy Press, 1982

Munitz, Milton K., *Space, Time and Creation: Philosophical Aspects of Scientific Cosmology*, Glencoe: Free Press, 1957.

______ *The Mystery of Existence: An Essay in Philosophical Cosmology*, New York: Appleton-Century-Crofts, 1965.

Murphy, Nancey C., "Does Prayer Make a Difference", *Cosmos as Creation: Theology and Science in Consonance* (ed. Ted Peters), Nashville: Abingdon Press, 1989.

Muslim, ibn Ḥajjāj, *al-Jāmi' al-ṣaḥīḥ*, Cairo, 1991.

Nasafī, Abū al-Mu'īn al-, *Baḥr al-kalām fī 'aqāid ahl al-Islām*, Konya, 1329.

______ *Tabṣira al-adilla fī uṣūl al-dīn* (ed. Claude Salame), Damascus, 1993.

______ *al-Tamhīd fī uṣūl al-dīn* (ed. 'Abd al-Ḥayy Qābil), Cairo: Dār al-thaqāfa, 1987.

Nasafī, 'Azīz al-dīn al-, Insan-i Kamil (tr. to Turkish: Mehmet Kanar), Istanbul: Dergah, 1990.

Nasaī, Aḥmad ibn Shu'ayb al-, *al-Sunan*, Beirut, 1930.

Nasr, Seyyed Hossein, *Knowledge and the Sacred*, Albany: State University of New York, 1989.

_____ *Man and Nature: The Spiritual Crisis of Modern Man*, Kuala Lumpur Foundation for Traditional Studies, 1986.

_____ *Religion and the Order of Nature*, New York and Oxford: Oxford University Press, 1996.

Nawawī, Yaḥyā ibn Sharaf al-, *Ḥilya al-abrār wa shi'ār al-akhyār* (ed. 'Alī al-Shurbajī, Qāsim al-Nūrī), Beirut: Risāla, 1992.

Nielsen, Kai, *Naturalism without Foundations*, New York: Prometheus Books, 1996.

Nursi, Said, *al-Mathnawī al-'arabī al-nūrī*, Istanbul: Sözler, 1999.

Olding, Alan, *Modern Biology and Natural Theology*, London and New York: Routledge, 1991.

Olson, Eric T., *The Human Animal: Personal Identity without Psychology*, New York: Oxford University Press, 1997.

Oparin, A. I., *The Origin of Life on the Earth* (tr. Ann Synge), Edinburgh: Oliver and Boyd, 1957.

O'Shaughnessy, Thomas J., *Creation and the Teaching of the Qur'an*, Rome: Biblical Institute Press, 1985.

Otto, Rudolf, *Naturalism and Religion* (tr. J. Arthur Thomson, Margaret R. Thomson), London: Williams & Norgate Ltd., 1907.

Parker, Barry, *Creation: The Story of the Origin and Evolution of the Universe*, New York and London: Plenum Press, 1988.

Peacocke, Arthur, *Creation and the World of Science: The Bampton Lectures 1978*, New York: Oxford University Press, 1979.

Pearl, Judea, *Causality: Models, Reasoning, and Inference*, New York: Cambridge University Press, 2000.

Peat, F. David, *Synchronicity: The Bridge Between Matter and Mind*, New York: Bantam Books, 1987.

Peters, Karl E., *Dancing with the Sacred: Evolution, Ecology and God*, Harrisburg: Trinity Press International, 2002.

Plato, *Timaeus* (tr. Benjamin Jowett), Rockville, Maryland: Serenity Publishers, LLC, 2009.

Plotinus, *The Enneads* (tr. Stephen MacKenna), Burdett, New York: Larson Publications, 1992.

Polkinghorne, John, *Belief in God in an Age of Science*, New Haven and London: Yale University Press, 1998.

_____ *Beyond Science: The Wider Human Context*, New York: Cambridge University Press, 1998.

_____ *Faith, Science and Understanding*, New Haven and London: Yale University Press, 2000.

_____ *Science and Providence: God's Interaction with the World*, Boston: New Science Library, Shambhala, 1989.

_____ *Science and Theology: An Introduction*, Minneapolis: Fortress Press, 1998.

Popper, Karl R., *The Open Universe: An Argument for Indeterminism* (ed. W. W. Bartley, III), Totowa, New Jersey: Rowman and Littlefield, 1982.

Qāḍī 'Abd al-Jabbār al-, *al-Mughnī fī abwāb al-tawḥīd wa al-'adl*, Cairo, undated.

_____ *al-Muḥīt bi al-taklīf* (ed. 'Umar al-Sayyid 'Azmī), Cairo, undated.

_____ *Sharḥ al-Uṣūl al-Khamsa* (ed. 'Abd al-Karīm 'Uthmān), Cairo, 1965.

Qunawī, Ṣadruddīn al-, *Fatiha Suresi Tefsiri* (tr. to Turkish: Ekrem Demirli), Istanbul: Iz, 2002.

Qushayrī, 'Abd al-Karīm ibn Hawāzin al-, *al-Risāla al-Qushayriyya fī 'ilm al-taṣawwuf*, Beirut: Dār al-khayr, 1993.

Rāghib al-Isfahānī, *al-I'tiqādāt*, Beirut, 1988.

_____ *al-Mufradāt fī gharīb al-Qur'ān*, Beirut, 1998.

_____ *Tafṣīl al-nash'atayn wa taḥṣīl al-sa'ādatayn*, (ed. 'Abd al-Majīd al-Najjār), Beirut: Dār al-Gharb al-Islāmī, 1988.

Rahman, Fazlur, *Major Themes of the Qur'an*, Minneapolis: Bibliotheca Islamica, 1994.

Rāzī, Fakhr al-dīn al-, *al-Arba'īn fī uṣūl al-dīn* (ed. Aḥmad Hijāzī), Cairo: Maktaba al-kulliyyāt al-Azhariyya, 1986.

_____ *I'tiqādāt firaq al-muslimīn wa al-mushrikīn*, Beirut, 1982.

_____ *al-Qaḍā' wa al-qadar*, Beirut, 1990.

_____ *Kitāb Lawāmi' al-bayyināt*, Egypt: al-Maṭba'a al-Sharafiyya, 1323.

_____ *Kitāb Ma'ālim uṣūl al-dīn*, Beirut, 1992.

_____ *al-Mabāḥith al-mashriqiyya fī 'ilm al-ilāhiyyāt wa al-ṭabī'iyyāt*, Beirut, 1990.

_____ *al-Masāil al-khamsūn fī uṣūl al-dīn* (ed. Aḥmad Hijāzī), Cairo: al-Maktaba al-thaqafī, 1989.

_____ *al-Nubuwwāt wa mā yata'allaq bihā*, Beirut, 1986.

_____ *al-Tafsīr al-kabīr*, Beirut: Dār al-kutub al-'ilmiyya, 1990.

Rea, Michael C., *World without Design: The Ontological Consequences of Naturalism*, Oxford: Clarendon Press, 2002.

Recanati, François, *Meaning and Force: The Pragmatics of Performative Utterances*, New York: Cambridge University Press, 1987.

Reck, Andrew J., *Speculative Philosophy: A Study of Its Nature, Types and Uses*, Albuquerque: The University of New Mexico Press, 1972.

Reid, Robert G. B., *Biological Emergences: Evolution by Natural Experiment*, Cambridge, Massachusetts: MIT Press, 2007.

Rescher, Nicholas, *Complexity: A Philosophical Overview*, New Brunswick, New Jersey: Transaction Publishers, 1998.

Rogers, John J. W., *A History of the Earth*, Cambridge: Cambridge University Press, 1994.

Root, Howard, "Metaphysics and Religious Belief", *Prospect for Metaphysics: Essays of Metaphysical Exploration* (ed. Ian Ramsey), New York: Philosophical Library, 1961.

Rosenberg, Alex, *Philosophy of Science: A Contemporary Introduction*, New York and London: Routledge, 2005.

Roy, M. N., *Materialism*, Delhi: Ajanta Publications, 1982.

Rucker, Rudy, *Infinity and the Mind: The Science and Philosophy of the Infinite*, Boston, 1982.

Ruse, Michael, *Evolutionary Naturalism*, New York: Routledge, 1995.

______ *The Evolution-Creation Struggle*, Cambridge: Harvard University Press, 2005.

Ryan, Frank, *Darwin's Blind Spot: Evolution Beyond Natural Selection*, Boston and New York: Houghton Mifflin Company, 2002.

Ṣābūnī, Nūr al-dīn al-, *al-Bidāya fī uṣūl al-dīn* (ed. Bekir Topaloğlu), Ankara, 1995.

Sagan, Carl, *The Demon-Haunted World: Science as a Candle in the Dark*, New York: Random House, 1995.

Sarakhsī, Muḥammad ibn Aḥmad al-, *Uṣūl*, Beirut: Dār al-ma'rifa, 1973.

Sarrāj, Abū Naṣr, *al-Luma'*, Egypt, 1960.

Sattig, Thomas, *The Language and Reality of Time*, Oxford: Clarendon Press, 2006.

Saunders, Nicholas, *Divine Action and Modern Science*, Cambridge: Cambridge University Press, 2002.

Schneider, Herbert W., "The Unnatural", *Naturalism and the Human Spirit* (ed. Yervant H. Krikorian), New York: Columbia University Press, 1945.

Schopenhauer, Arthur, *The World as Will and Representation* (tr. E. F. J. Payne), Massachusetts: The Falcon's Wing Press, 1958.

Schroeder, Gerald L., *The Hidden Face of God: How Science Reveals the Ultimate Truth*, New York: The Free Press, 2001.

Schrödinger, Erwin, *What is Life: The Physical Aspect of the Living Cell*, Cambridge: Cambridge University Press, 2008.

Schwartz, Jeffrey H., *Sudden Origins: Fossils, Genes, and the Emergence of Species*, New York: John Wiley and Sons, 1999.

Schwarz, Hans, *Creation*, Grand Rapids, Michigan: William B. Eerdmans Publishing, 2002.

Sellars, Roy Wood, *Evolutionary Naturalism*, New York: Russell & Russell, 1969.

Shahristānī, Muḥammad ibn 'Abd al-Karīm al-, *Nihāya al-aqdām fī 'ilm al-kalām* (ed. Alfred Guillaume), Oxford, 1934.

Shattuck, Cybelle, *Hinduism*, New Jersey: Prentice Hall, 1999.

Sidharth, B. G., *The Chaotic Universe: From Planck to the Hubble Scale*, Huntington, New York: Nova Science Publishers, 2001.

Silk, Joseph, *On the Shores of the Unknown: A Short History of the Universe*, New York: Cambridge University Press, 2005.

______ *The Big Bang*, New York: W. H. Freeman and Company, 2001.

Smedes, Taede A., *Chaos, Complexity, and God: Divine Action and Scientism*, Leuven, Paris, Dudley: Peeters, 2004.

Smith, A. D., "Non-Reductive Physicalism?", *Objections to Physicalism* (ed. Howard Robinson), Oxford: Oxford University Press, 1993.

Smith, Wilfred Cantwell, *Faith and Belief*, New Jersey: Princeton University Press, 1979.

______ *What is Scripture: A Comparative Approach*, Minneapolis: Fortress Press, 1993.

Sorley, William Ritchie, *The Ethics of Naturalism: A Criticism*, New York: Books for Libraries Press, 1969.

Southwood, T. R. E., *The Story of Life*, Oxford: Oxford University Press, 2003.

Spence, Lewis, *Introduction to Mytology*, London: Senate, 1994.

Stace, W. T., *The Nature of the World: An Essay in Phenomenalist Metaphysics*, Princeton: Princeton University Press, 1940.

Stewart, Ian, *Does God Play Dice?: The Mathematics of Chaos*, Oxford and New York: Basil Blackwell, 1989.

______ *Nature's Numbers: The Unreal Reality of Mathematics*, New York: BasicBooks, 1995.

Subkī, 'Abd al-wahhāb ibn 'Alī, al-, *al-Sayf al-mashhūr fī sharḥ 'Aqīda Abī Manṣūr*, (ed. M. Saim Yeprem), Istanbul, 1989.

Taftāzānī, Ṣa'd al-dīn al-, *Sharḥ al-'Aqāid al-Nasafiyya*, Istanbul, undated.

______ *Sharḥ al-Maqāṣid*, Istanbul, 1277.

Tarbuck, Edward J., Frederick K. Lutgens, *Earth Science*, Upper Saddle River, New Jersey: Prentice Hall, 2000.

Taylor, Richard, *Metaphysics*, New Jersey: Prentice-Hall, 1983.

Taylor, Stuart Ross, *Solar System Evolution: A New Perspective*, Cambridge: Cambridge University Press, 2001.

Tirmidhī, Muḥammad ibn Īsā, *al-Jāmi' al-ṣaḥīḥ*, Egypt, 1975.

Tolstoy, Leo, *Confession* (tr. David Patterson), New York: W. W. Norton & Company, 1996.

Torrance, Robert M., *The Spiritual Quest: Transcendence in Myth, Religion, and Science*, Berkeley and Los Angeles: University of California Press, 1994.

Toulmin, Stephen, "Contemporary Scientific Mythology", *Metaphysical Beliefs* (ed. Stephen Toulmin, Ronald W. Hepburn, Alasdair MacIntyre), New York: Schocken Books, 1970.

_____ *Cosmopolis: The Hidden Agenda of Modernity*, New York: The Free Press, 1990.

Tudge, Colin, *The Veriety of Life: A Survey and a Celebration of All the Creatures that Have Ever Lived*, Oxford: Oxford University Press, 2000.

Usmandī, Muḥammad ibn 'Abd al-Ḥamīd al-, *Lubāb al-kalām* (ed. M. Sait Özer-varli), Istanbul, 1998.

Walker, Ralph, "Transcendental Arguments against Physicalism", *Objections to Physicalism* (ed. Howard Robinson), Oxford: Oxford University Press, 1993.

Weiss, Paul, *Being and Other Realities*, Chicago and La Salle, Illinois: Open Court, 1995.

Westerhoff, Jan, *Ontological Categories: Their Nature and Significance*, New York: Oxford University Press, 2005.

Westfall, Richard S., *The Construction of Modern Science: Mechanism and Mechanics*, Cambridge: Cambridge University Press, 1980.

White, Vernon, *The Fall of a Sparrow: A Concept of Special Divine Action*, Exeter: The Paternoster Press, 1985.

Whitehead, Alfred North, *Process and Reality: An Essay in Cosmology* (ed. David Ray Griffin, Donald W. Sherburne), New York: The Free Press, 1978.

_____ *The Concept of Nature*, Cambridge: Cambridge University Press, 1964.

Wicander, Reed, James S. Monroe, *Essentials of Geology*, Belmont, California: Wadsworth Publishing Company, 1999.

_____ and James S. Monroe, *Historical Geology: Evolution of Earth and Life through Time*, Belmont, California: Thomson Brooks/Cole, 2003.

Wilson, Edvard O., *The Diversity of Life*, New York and London: W. W. Norton & Company, 1993.

Witherall, Arthur, *The Problem of Existence*, Hants: Ashgate, 2002.

Wittgenstein, Ludwig, *Tractatus Logico-Philosophicus* (tr. D. F. Pears, B. F. McGuinness), London: Routledge & Kegan Paul, 1961.

Zabīdī, Muḥammad Murtaḍā ibn Muḥammad al-, *Tāj al-'arūs min jawāhir al-Qāmūs*, undated.

Zajjāj, Abū Isḥāq al-, *Tafsīr asmā' Allāh al-ḥusnā* (ed. Aḥmad Yūsuf), Damascus: Dār al-ma'mūn li al-turāth, 1986.

Zajjājī, 'Abd al-Raḥmān ibn Isḥāq al-, *Ishtiqāq asmā' Allāh*, Beirut: Muassasa al-Risāla, 1986.

INDEX

A

B

C

D

E

F

G

H

I

N

O

P

Q

R

S

T

U

V

W

Y

Z